Poetry Tables

PRAISE FOR *POETRY TABLES*

"The poet William Carlos Williams wrote, 'It is difficult to get the news from a poem. But men die miserably every day for lack of what is to be found there.' David Markwardt's work and his book, *Poetry Tables*, are commitments to bringing the value of poetry into our world. *Poetry Tables* is an invaluable resource for facilitators and teachers who are looking for ways to deeply touch the human spirit. Today, more than ever, this is important work!"

Hersch Wilson, author of Firefighter Zen: A Handbook for Thriving in Tough Times.

"David introduced me to Poetry Tables years ago. Since then, I have used them many times in my work. The process of reading and discovering a poem that speaks to you frees us from analytic mind and takes us into the realm of emotions, memories, longings, and experiences. Poetry Tables never fail to support us into a fuller expression of who we are. Done with colleagues and strangers, this process brings us together in new, revealing, and productive ways."

Margaret Wheatley, author of Leadership and the New Science
and Who Do We Choose to Be?

"David Markwardt is an unusually gifted poet and organization consultant—a rare and powerful combination. David helps organizations get to the root of the issues that confront them. He's able to go deep fast, always with respect for his clients' needs. Through the portal of poetry and using his clear understanding of how people learn and change, David makes magic happen in the workplace. I recommend him enthusiastically—for his capacity to move people and, more importantly, for his ability to help people move themselves.

Leslie Osborn, Executive Coach

"I was fortunate to have David Markwardt introduce Poetry Tables to our team when I served as the Executive Director of the Banff Centre's Leadership Development Programmes. Experiencing it, I came to appreciate that Poetry Tables aren't about poetry for poetry's sake; rather, they are about *learning through poetry*. Markwardt has masterfully designed a process where poetry is not an ends but rather a means, a tool for connecting and building community. In our engagement with Poetry Tables, the poems became a catalyst for a conversation—a conversation about whatever mattered. It afforded us language where other words fell short, and allowed us to get 'unstuck.' Best of all, our imaginations were stirred—new language afforded us new possibilities. Poetry Tables are one of the best art-based learning activities I have seen."

Nick Nissley, Ed.D., President, Northwestern Michigan College

"A Poetry Table is a great vehicle for gaining insight about roles, goals, and challenges in the workplace. It opens a level of communication between participants that is profound and provocative without crossing into the realm of being too personal an interaction for coworkers. The knowledge that I gained about myself will serve me well in and out of the office. It helped me understand my fellow participants and their needs in a way I had not anticipated. I would recommend this to any organization that is seeking to foster greater understanding and cooperation among coworkers. It is better than any other team-building exercise that I have taken part in."

Elisabeth Keller, Learning Specialist

Poetry Tables

How to Create Profound Experiences of

Courage, Connection, and Community

Using Poetry

An Introduction for Organizational Development
Consultants, Teachers, Therapists, and Team Leaders

David B. Markwardt

CONTENTS

FACILITATION

APPENDIX

Red Brocade

The Arabs used to say
When a stranger appears at your door,
feed him for three days
before asking who he is,
where he's come from,
where's he headed.
That way, he'll have strength
enough to answer.
Or, by then you'll be
such good friends
you don't care.

Let's go back to that.
Rice? Pine nuts?
Here, take the red brocade pillow.
My child will serve water
to your horse.

No, I was not busy when you came!
I was not preparing to be busy.
That's the armor everyone put on
to pretend they had a purpose
in the world.

I refuse to be claimed.
Your plate is waiting.
We will snip fresh mint
into your tea.

Naomi Shihab Nye

Yes, indeed, "let's go back to that!" In a world of disconnection and division, let's take off the armor and return to a world of hospitality, graciousness, and connection.

Welcome to a book about poetry and the power of Poetry Tables. As the name implies, during a Poetry Table you sit at a table. On the table are a stack of eighty to ninety poems. You sit in a small group and read the poems in silence, setting aside poems that you like. Afterwards, you choose one and read it aloud to your small group and speak about why it matters to you. It is a surprising, intimate, and revealing experience.

This book shares profound personal stories and explains how to design Poetry Tables. It is targeted at facilitators, trainers, therapists, and teachers who are looking for a novel way of opening up individuals and groups, and connecting people. The intention is for interested educators, change agents, and interventionists to understand the process, be intrigued enough to want to try it for their team or class, and then either sponsor a Poetry Table or facilitate one themselves.

A Poetry Table is a versatile tool that can be used in innumerable settings and contexts. It can be adapted to address countless outcomes, which I'll explain throughout the book.

Poetry experienced through a Poetry Table can be a door into the dark or a window into the light. It can create a greater range of feeling, inner expansiveness, and aliveness, and it can connect, heal, inspire, and sustain you. It can connect you to your heart, encourage you to be courageous, and can change, even transform, your life.

But more than saving individual selves, poetry may save us—our societies and communities. During World War II, the great Polish poet Czeslaw Milosz asked in his poem, "Dedication,"

> What is poetry which does not save
> Nations or people?

Milosz's expectation of poetry's potential power and its moral imperative to save humanity is aspirational, timeless, and noble.

The mission of Poetry Tables is to save humanity—a tall order.

> Ah, but a man's reach should exceed his grasp,
> Or what's a heaven for?
>
> From "Andrea del Sarto" by Robert Browning

Any poem could be appropriate for a Poetry Table depending on the context. I've only used some of the poems in this book in Poetry Tables. Others are waiting for their opportunity! More about how to choose poems is presented in chapter 16.

The book is accessible to anyone interested in learning through poetry. Whether you are a professional working with people or just a curious human, reading this book may make you slow down to savor the poems, reflect, and then reach out and share them with friends and family.

CHAPTER 1

Cutting Through Our Defenses

A FEW YEARS AGO, I facilitated a retreat in Colorado for the human resources group of an organization that runs many ski areas in North America. Asked to choose from a stack of poems, a manager in his small group picked David Wagoner's "Lost."

Lost

Stand still. The trees ahead and bushes beside you
Are not lost. Wherever you are is called Here,
And you must treat it as a powerful stranger,
Must ask permission to know it and be known.
The forest breathes. Listen. It answers,
I have made this place around you,
If you leave it you may come back again, saying Here.
No two trees are the same to Raven.
No two branches are the same to Wren.
If what a tree or a bush does is lost on you,
You are surely lost. Stand still. The forest knows
Where you are. You must let it find you.

David Wagoner

It was a profound poem for the manager and shook him deeply. He realized he was unsure of what to do next, where to go in his life, what job direction to take. He was at a crossroads and needed, wanted, to make a career move, but didn't know which way to go. The poem spoke for where he was and offered a suggestion on what he could do. Instead of the conventional wisdom of "Don't just sit there, do something," the poem suggests—do nothing. "Stand still. The forest knows/ Where you are. You must let it find you."

He emailed me a few months later to let me know that, after a period of reflection, he quit his job and started his own graphic design consulting business, something he had been dreaming about doing for years.

The human resources manager's story is typical for a Poetry Table. Poetry has a way of cutting through our defenses and touching our depths. It also has a way of offering fresh perspectives. It provides insight and clarity. It may move people to action.

Not every Poetry Table contains profound moments. As a skeptical person, I appreciate critical thought and doubt. For the skeptical reader, I don't want to guarantee a profound experience. However, I will guarantee depth if a Poetry Table is facilitated well. Even if a Poetry Table doesn't touch a profound place, it reliably reaches a deep place. For example, I facilitated a Poetry Table in March 2022 with a leadership group that I had already been working with for six months. Here are sample comments from the evaluations:

- "The poetry exercise allowed us to get to know each other on a deeper level."
- "The poetry reading and reflection offered a different lens from which to look through to get to know one another."
- "The poetry exercise provided a vehicle to discuss our personal concerns and professional issues through a different medium."

- "I thought the poetry activity was very insightful and brought out different skills we may not recognize on a daily basis."
- "I'm not much into poetry, but the exercise allowed me to know my group even better."
- "The connection event over the poetry was a really unique way to come together and talk about how the poem intersects in our lives."
- "The poem exercise was very valuable. It brought out different perspectives than some classmates previously expressed."

The above comments are typical for every Poetry Table.

As a facilitator, poet, leadership trainer, and former teacher, I've looked at the value of a Poetry Table experience through many lenses and will share those with you, so you can quickly find the ones that resonate with you as a practitioner and poetry reader yourself. Most facilitators, teachers, coaches, and therapists have a certain emotional concept in mind when working with their participants. While we cannot predict why people will be drawn to certain poems and metaphorical ideas, here are some concepts that I have witnessed my participants connect with:

- Flow
- Soul and life's path ("Gradient"– more on this in chapter 6)
- Grief
- Kindness
- Parenting
- Leading
- Drawing out ("*Educare*" – more on this in chapter 8)
- Change
- Awe

I have facilitated Poetry Tables with all kinds of groups: a classroom of seven-year-old students at a Montessori school; leaders in corporate and community leadership programs; for-profit, non-profit, public benefit, and governmental organizations at all levels; water treatment operators; and construction managers. I have seen the incredible impact reading and talking about poems has had on people and how it has changed lives. In an instant, individuals have had epiphanies and relationships have been transformed. This book is about their stories, why poetry matters, and how facilitators, trainers, therapists, and teachers can create profound Poetry Table experiences.

The book is organized in the following way:

- Chapter 2 offers a definition of poetry, which may be different than the one you immediately think of.
- Chapter 3 gives a more detailed explanation of what a Poetry Table is.
- Chapter 4 tells Poetry Table stories from a diverse range of people.
- Chapter 5 tells about the author and how Poetry Tables came to be.
- Chapters 6 and 7 touch upon key elements of individual and collective discovery.
- Chapter 8 addresses different ways of learning.
- Chapter 9–12 looks more deeply at key elements of what poetry has to offer.
- Chapters 13–18 are the specific "how to." They are the manual.
- Chapter 19 addresses two sample outcomes, though I could address many, many more.
- Chapter 20 fittingly ends with a poem.

CHAPTER 2

What Is Poetry?

POET EDWARD HIRSCH SAYS poetry "is necessary speech." I've also heard it defined as "heartfelt speech." Poet Emily Dickinson says poetry is infinite possibility, which is how I experience poetry.

I dwell in Possibility – (466)

I dwell in Possibility –
A fairer house than Prose –
More numerous of Windows –
Superior – for Doors –

Of Chambers as the Cedars –
Impregnable of eye –
And for an everlasting Roof –
The Gambrels of the Sky –

Of Visitors – the fairest–
For Occupation – This –
The spreading wide my narrow Hands
To gather Paradise –

Emily Dickinson

What draws me to "I dwell in Possibility," besides its compact lines and high energy, is its expansiveness and its boundless belief in the alchemy between poetic language and the imagination.

Polish poet and Nobel Prize in Literature winner Wislawa Szymborska professes not to know what poetry is in the following witty poem.

Some People Like Poetry

Some people—
that means not everyone.
Not even most of them, only a few.
Not counting school, where you have to,
and poets themselves,
you might end up with something like two per thousand.

Like—
but then, you can like chicken noodle soup,
or compliments, or the color blue,
your old scarf,
your own way,
petting the dog.

Poetry—
but what is poetry anyway?
More than one rickety answer
has tumbled since that question first was raised.
But I just keep on not knowing, and I cling to that
like a redemptive handrail.

Wislawa Szymborska

What draws me to "Some People Like Poetry" is its dry wit and edgy truth about poetry's relative minor place in the average person's life. And yet, I like how she suggests that poetry sometimes breaks through the mundane and possibly redeems some people.

I am one of those people. As a person with low material wants but high spiritual needs, I value the spiritual lift and beauty of truth that poetry brings. I am a better husband, father, and human by reading poetry. Poetry offers redemption and is, indeed, a redemptive handrail.

What Is a Poetry Table?

DURING A POETRY TABLE, you sit in a small group of three to five people. For approximately ten minutes, you read in silence and at your own speed poems from a stack of eighty to ninety poems set on the table. As you read, you put aside poems that you like and that matter to you. If you don't like a poem, you put it back in the middle of the table for other people to read.

After that, you receive the Invitation Sheet inviting you to pick a poem from your personal stack, read it twice aloud in your small group, and answer the following four questions:

- "What initially drew you to the poem?"
- "What words, lines, and images stand out for you from the poem?"
- "What about the poem matters to you? Why did you pick it?"
- "How does the poem intersect with your life and work?"

People take turns reading, answering the questions, sharing, and exchanging stories, ideas, and views.

After that, the small groups reconvene as a large group. A few people are invited to read their poems, discuss their answers to the above-mentioned questions, and share their personal connections to their poems. Sharing in the large group, making the private public, takes daring and courage, and it is often extraordinarily powerful. It can be a sacred communal moment.

There's more to the activity than this description, which I'll detail in the Facilitation section in chapters 13, 14, 15, 16, 17, 18, and 19.

CHAPTER 4

Profound Experiences

"For poems are not, as people think, simply emotions
(one has emotions early enough)—they are experiences."

Rainer Maria Rilke

THE FOLLOWING STORIES ARE about people experiencing the power of poetry and how it touched their lives. The names of the people are fictitious.

Several years ago, I was invited to facilitate a Poetry Table for a group of managers in a leadership program for a construction company. The company built large structures like embassies and highway interchanges. The conference was at a resort in Texas. Charlie picked "Courage" by Anne Sexton.

Courage

It is in the small things we see it.
The child's first step,
as awesome as an earthquake.
The first time you rode a bike,
wallowing up the sidewalk.

The first spanking when your heart
went on a journey all alone.
When they called you crybaby
or poor or fatty or crazy
and made you into an alien,
you drank their acid
and concealed it.

Later,
If you faced the death of bombs and bullets
you did not do it with a banner,
you did it with only a hat to
cover your heart.
You did not fondle the weakness inside you
though it was there.
Your courage was a small coal
that you kept swallowing.
If your buddy saved you
and died himself in so doing,
then his courage was not courage,
it was love; love as simple as shaving soap.

Later,
if you have endured a great despair,
then you did it alone
getting a transfusion from the fire,
picking the scabs off your heart,
then wringing it out like a sock.
Next, my kinsman, you powdered your sorrow,
you gave it a back rub
and then you covered it with a blanket
and after it had slept a while
it woke to the wings of the roses
and was transformed.

Later,
when you face old age and its natural conclusion
your courage will still be shown in the little ways,

each spring will be a sword you'll sharpen,
those you love will live in a fever of love,
and you'll bargain with the calendar
and at the last moment
when death opens the back door
you'll put on your carpet slippers
and stride out.

Anne Sexton

After small-group conversations, when we reconvened as a large group, I asked if anyone wanted to read their poem, share why it mattered, why they picked it, and how it related to their life and work. Charlie volunteered to read "Courage" and then told the group he had lost a daughter in a car accident. The third stanza was about the great despair; the strong imagery and the transformation of grief had touched him and hooked him. He could relate to that experience of grief and transformation. Charlie repeated multiple times how much he really loved the poem and how healing it was for him. It allowed him to express his most potent, pent-up emotions and release them.

LIFE IS ENERGY AND ENERGY IS CREATIVITY

The poet Marianne Moore said, "Life is energy and energy is creativity. And even when individuals pass on, the energy is retained in the work of art, locked in it and awaiting release if only someone will take the time and the care to unlock it." Anne Sexton died in 1974. The energy of her poem survived for the construction manager to unlock it thirty-seven years later during the leadership program in June 2011. Reading "Courage" long after she wrote it, Charlie experienced its energy and power to heal. Image after image and line after line released energy in him to acknowledge his sorrow and loss.

That is what happens when you connect with a poem. A blocked area in you becomes unblocked. A wound opens to the light. You feel energized. You feel alive. Your imagination is stirred. You imagine possibilities, a different future, a new way of being. You feel the energy to be creative and are motivated to take action. This is a unique type of genius of which, without exception, every human is capable.

At the same leadership program where Charlie picked "Courage," Randy picked "Kindness" by Naomi Shihab Nye.

Kindness

Before you know what kindness really is
you must lose things,
feel the future dissolve in a moment
like salt in a weakened broth.
What you held in your hand,
what you counted and carefully saved,
all this must go so you know
how desolate the landscape can be
between the regions of kindness.
How you ride and ride
thinking the bus will never stop,
the passengers eating maize and chicken
will stare out the window forever.

Before you learn the tender gravity of kindness
you must travel where the Indian in a white poncho
lies dead by the side of the road.
You must see how this could be you,
how he too was someone
who journeyed through the night with plans
and the simple breath that kept him alive.

Before you know kindness as the deepest thing inside,

you must know sorrow as the other deepest thing.
You must wake up with sorrow.
You must speak to it till your voice
catches the thread of all sorrows
and you see the size of the cloth.
Then it is only kindness that makes sense anymore,
only kindness that ties your shoes
and sends you out into the day to gaze at bread,
only kindness that raises its head
from the crowd of the world to say
It is I you have been looking for,
and then goes with you everywhere
like a shadow or a friend.

Naomi Shihab Nye

Randy was a tall, bald, big guy and looked intimidating, like a state trooper at a traffic stop. He told the large group he managed by fear, by intimidating people, and he had come, over time, to realize the limits and shortcomings to his method. He wasn't approachable nor empathetic. His staff was afraid to ask him questions and be vulnerable with him. Randy admitted his way of managing wasn't working anymore for him as a manager or as a person. It had taken him far, but not far enough. He wasn't getting the positive results he wanted with people and didn't like the person he had become. He wanted to have a better balance, to be kinder and more empathetic. The poem reminded him of how he wanted to be.

Sometimes people pick the same poem for different reasons. During a community leadership program in January 2018, an engineer with a utility company also picked "Kindness." Fred was quiet and reserved, very introverted, and friendly in one-on-one conversations, but he never said anything in the large group.

Fred read "Kindness" to his leadership class of thirty. He said he chose it because his only son had died by suicide and the poem was healing for him. He was drawn to the opening lines:

> Before you know what kindness really is
> you must lose things,
> feel the future dissolve in a moment
> like salt in a weakened broth.
> What you held in your hand,
> what you counted and carefully saved,
> all this must go so you know
> how desolate the landscape can be
> between the regions of kindness.

Fred talked about how hard his son's death was on him. Everyone in the group was stunned at what he had to say. I remember a collective gasp and a "holy shit." It was so unexpected. He didn't say much. In some ways, he was matter-of-fact about his loss, but everyone could feel his pain. His few words were extremely powerful. His sharing was an honest, raw, courageous act. It gave him a voice and illuminated for others the deeper meaning of the poem.

THE TABLE METAPHOR

The table metaphor is a rich and vibrant one. It is inviting, welcoming, and a place to feast. A Poetry Table can be offered. A Poetry Table can be "set."

A Poetry Table can be set with all ages, even with children. In 2012, I facilitated one with my son's second grade class at his Montessori school. One girl picked "Don't Quit." The poem has been attributed to different people. Here is a version.

Don't Quit

When things go wrong, as they sometimes will,
When the road you're trudging seems all uphill,
When the funds are low and the debts are high,
And you want to smile, but you have to sigh,
When care is pressing you down a bit,
Rest, if you must – but don't you quit!
Life is queer with its twists and turns,
As every one of us sometimes learns,
And many a failure turns about
When he might have won had he stuck it out;
Don't give up though the pace seems slow –
You may succeed with another blow.
Often the goal is nearer than
It seems to a faint and faltering man;
Often the struggler has given up
When he might have captured the victor's cup;
And he learned too late when the night came down,
How close he was to the golden crown.
Success is failure turned inside out –
The silver tint in the clouds of doubt,
And you never can tell how close you are,
It might be near when it seems afar;
So stick to the fight when you're hardest hit –
It's when things seem worst that you must not quit.

Unknown

At her young age, Violet had already had multiple surgeries for birth defects. It was powerful to hear her read the poem first to her small group and then to the entire class, and talk about why she picked it and why it mattered to her. Her teachers and I were barely holding back tears as she spoke. It celebrated her persistence and gave her classmates a window into her struggles.

Not all stories that emerge from Poetry Tables are about sorrow and grief. Communicating the things of which we are afraid or ashamed, or that we deeply care about or love, is not easy. When we share them and bring the private public, or choose to reveal what is secret and hidden, we may feel relief, freedom, and even joy. We can feel less isolated and more connected, and experience a sense of belonging.

The act of speaking about the things that are hard for us can be liberating, not only for the speaker but also for everyone present. The weight is lifted. Speaking about our own helplessness and ignorance often allows joy to emerge in the room. People laugh at our common humanity. We are all flawed humans. When people share their humanity in a Poetry Table, it can be an incredibly liberating experience. Trust goes up. Communication is a success. People are more connected.

Life is a never-ending cycle of connection and disconnection, and of communication and miscommunication. A Poetry Table can provide a rare moment of deep connection and authentic communication. We can say "I can trust you" because we know the other person isn't faking it. They are being genuine and authentic.

Poet Czeslaw Milosz said in his essay, "My Intention,"

> Each of us is so ashamed of his own helplessness and ignorance that he considers it appropriate to communicate only what he thinks others will understand. There are, however, times when somehow we slowly divest ourselves of that shame and begin to speak openly about all the things we do not understand. If I am not wise, then why must I pretend to be? If I am lost, why must I pretend to have ready counsel for my contemporaries? But perhaps the value of communication depends on the acknowledgment of one's own limits, which, mysteriously, are also limits common to many others; and aren't these the same limits of a hundred thousand years ago? And when the air is

filled with the clamor of analysis and conclusion, would it be entirely useless to admit you do not understand?[1]

A poem can be a type of talisman. On another occasion, I led a Poetry Table at a leadership conference at a ski resort in Colorado. Through a Poetry Table, Eric rediscovered the poem "You Reading This Be Ready" by William Stafford. It had been folded up in his wallet for many years until the paper was shredded, worn out, and illegible. That poem meant something significant to him. By doing a Poetry Table, he rediscovered it.

You Reading This, Be Ready

Starting here, what do you want to remember?
How sunlight creeps along a shining floor?
What scent of old wood hovers, what softened
sound from outside fills the air?

Will you ever bring a better gift for the world
than the breathing respect that you carry
wherever you go right now? Are you waiting
for time to show you some better thoughts?

When you turn around, starting here, lift this
new glimpse that you found; carry into evening
all that you want from this day. This interval you spent
reading or hearing this, keep it for life—

What can anyone give you greater than now,
starting here, right in this room, when you turn around?

William Stafford

---

1. Czeslaw Milosz, "My Intention" from *To Begin Where I Am: Selected Essays* (New York: Farrar, Straus and Giroux, 2001), 1-3.

The poem mattered to Eric because it reminded him to be present, attentive, appreciative, and grateful for things in the present. He took a photo of the poem and now had a digital copy of his recovered talisman.

The most powerful experiences during a Poetry Table may be when people speak openly about feeling lost, helpless, ignorant, afraid, ashamed, vulnerable, and inadequate. When someone admits to being an imperfect human, expresses vulnerability, and admits to not having it all together, they often receive an incredible gift of healing.

One of my favorite examples of this was during a municipal leadership program when a police chief, wearing his uniform, looking polished and perfect, read Elizabeth Carlson's "Imperfection" to his small group and explained why it mattered to him. Later, at another session, Chief Ramon read the poem to the entire leadership class. He didn't hide that his appearance was a type of costume he put on to convey a message both of authority and reliability to his community. In fact, this was one of his messages throughout the class, that beneath the uniform, police officers are human, and his goal as chief was to bridge the divide between officers and citizens, creating opportunities for better relatedness. Admitting imperfection was one way of tackling the dual realities of his role.

Imperfection

I am falling in love
    with my imperfections
The way I never get the sink really clean,
forget to check my oil,
lose my car in parking lots,
miss appointments I have written down,
am just a little late.

I am learning to love
    the small bumps on my face
    the big bump of my nose,
    my hairless scalp,
chipped nail polish,
toes that overlap.
Learning to love
    the open-ended mystery
        of not knowing why

I am learning to fail
    to make lists,
use my time wisely,
    read the books I should.

Instead I practice inconsistency,
irrationality, forgetfulness.

Probably I should hang my clothes neatly in the closet
all the shirts together, then the pants,
send Christmas cards, or better yet
a letter telling of
my perfect family

But I'd rather waste time
listening to the rain,
or lying underneath my cat
    learning to purr.

I used to fill every moment
    with something I could
cross off later.

Perfect was
    the laundry done and folded
    all my papers graded
    the whole truth and nothing   but

Now the empty mind is what I seek

the formless shape
the strange   off center
sometimes fictional
                    me.

Elizabeth Carlson

A Poetry Table encourages people to take off their mask, the face they show to others, their persona. I recall a woman who worked in the development department of an art museum. Katie was as professional looking, polished, and perfect as the police chief. She picked "Now I Become Myself" by May Sarton.

Now I Become Myself

Now I become myself. It's taken
Time, many years and places;
I have been dissolved and shaken,
Worn other people's faces,
Run madly, as if Time were there,
Terribly old, crying a warning,
"Hurry, you will be dead before—"
(What? Before you reach the morning?
Or the end of the poem is clear?
Or love safe in the walled city?)
Now to stand still, to be here,
Feel my own weight and density!
The black shadow on the paper
Is my hand; the shadow of a word
As thought shapes the shaper
Falls heavy on the page, is heard.
All fuses now, falls into place
From wish to action, word to silence,
My work, my love, my time, my face
Gathered into one intense
Gesture of growing like a plant.

As slowly as the ripening fruit
Fertile, detached, and always spent,
Falls but does not exhaust the root,
So all the poem is, can give,
Grows in me to become the song,
Made so and rooted so by love.
Now there is time and Time is young.
O, in this single hour I live
All of myself and do not move.
I, the pursued, who madly ran,
Stand still, stand still, and stop the sun!

May Sarton

Up to that point in the community leadership program, Katie had appeared controlled. Some people in the class had a hard time relating to her. When she spoke about the poem in the large group, she said her life was at a crossroads. She was miserable in her prestigious job in the art world. Her work was no longer inspiring or had meaning for her. Katie wanted to quit. She was vulnerable, honest, open. She showed a human side of herself she hadn't in class. One classmate said that her openness completely changed how she saw her. After several months of being together, and multiple class sessions, the transformation in their relationship happened in an instant.

As it turned out, the poem and talking about it was the tipping point that encouraged her to take a risk and quit her position, even without a new job. Within a short time, a couple months, Katie found her dream job as development director at a nature organization, which was more in line with her values and passion for conserving the outdoors.

Another memorable story is about a sales director at a media company. He picked "I Am Not I" by Juan Ramon Jimenez. Eduardo picked it, in part, because life was precious to him. His younger sister had been murdered in New York City, and her death had a huge impact on him. He wanted to live as genuinely as possible and didn't want to waste time being fake. He recognized life could end any time, too soon. Eduardo later told me he downloaded a copy of his poem and taped it to his bathroom mirror to remind him before he walked out into the world that he wanted to go out the door being authentic. To be real.

I Am Not I

I am not I.
   I am this one
walking beside me whom I do not see,
whom at times I manage to visit,
and whom at other times I forget;
who remains calm and silent while I talk,
and forgives, gently, when I hate,
who walks where I am not,
who will remain standing when I die.

   Juan Ramon Jimenez

A Poetry Table experience can have a lasting impact on participants. In May 2021, while preparing for a team-building training for municipal employees, I reconnected with their manager who came to welcome them. Gino had taken a leadership program with me five years earlier. We started by catching up about what we had been doing and how we were faring with the Covid-19 pandemic. I told him I was writing a book about Poetry Table experiences. Immediately, Gino recalled his experience, the poem he had selected, and started telling me about its impact. Here is his poem. It is one of my own.

The Wolf at Two A.M.

Snapped awake
again, hail him with a smile and a slap

on his frizzled back.
He has come to remind –
anxiety is a favorite cousin
of being alive. Breathe his hot breath
till it blends with your own.
Ask permission to lick his snout.
Will he cower you into terror?
Will he tear you to shreds?
Escort him to your kitchen.
Whip up a meal,
whatever he wants. When you can look
unflinching in his piercing eyes, when so close
you see his jagged teeth are
your edge, you are close.
Open a bottle of wine.
Toast, clink glasses, laugh.
Belly laugh until dawn's breaking light.
If not this dark night then another.

David Markwardt

Even after five years, Gino vividly remembered words, lines, and images from the poem. "The Wolf of Anxiety," as he called it. He told me how reflecting on the poem had helped him manage the challenges of the Covid-19 pandemic. He spoke about trying to accept and embrace anxiety, befriend it, welcome it—have a glass of wine with it. Gino also told me how it had impacted his management style. He encouraged his staff not to run from anxiety, fear, and the challenges they were facing from the pandemic, and told them that to know anxiety is a part of life and being alive.

The right poem at the right time can spur action, insight, and imaginative thought. You could be in a rut and stuck looking at the world in the same old tired way. A poem can be a push. It can be a motivator to get up and go. It can be clarifying and put you on the spot.

Are you going to do something about this or not? The right poem at the right time can be consciousness-raising and action-inducing.

CHANGE

Archaic Torso of Apollo

We cannot know his legendary head
with eyes like ripening fruit. And yet his torso
is still suffused with brilliance from inside,
like a lamp, in which his gaze, now turned to low,
gleams in all its power. Otherwise
the curved breast could not dazzle you so, nor could
a smile run through the placid hips and thighs
to that dark center where procreation flared.
Otherwise this stone would seem defaced
beneath the translucent cascade of the shoulders
and would not glisten like a wild beast's fur:
would not, from all the borders of itself,
burst like a star: for here there is no place
that does not see you. You must change your life.

Rainer Maria Rilke

"There is no place that does not see you," Rilke writes at the end. "You must change your life." This is the ultimate challenge of a Poetry Table—to change your life and work. A moving poem doesn't just move your emotions. It moves you to action.

- Are you living with integrity?
- Are you living with purpose and meaning?
- Is your life joyful?

- Do you feel good about what you are doing and how you are living?
- Do you need to forgive someone? What would happen if you did?
- What do you want to do with your time?
- What are you called to be?
- What are you called to do?
- How are you called to lead?
- How could you be more intentional and lead with purpose?
- What values are present, or not, in your current role?

I could ask a hundred other questions with the power to provoke reflection that leads to change. The poem, the questions you're invited in a Poetry Table to consider, the new questions that arise as readers talk about their poems, as group members converse, all of these together create a synergistic, generative conversation that can lead anywhere and be transformative. All poems in Poetry Tables, in one way or another, ask you to reflect on and change your life and work.

People aren't used to encountering poetry the way they do in a Poetry Table, nor are they used to encountering the request to change their lives and work! And changing your life, of course, changes how you lead, love, follow. The artificial barriers between work and life break down.

I am reclaiming poetry and inviting you to reclaim it as a birthright and as a source of wisdom and delight. Poetry is one of so many things that formal education has stripped from us. Typically, students are asked in school to read a poem their teacher has picked for them, then analyze it, discussing what the poem means—not to them as individuals, but generically. This approach often alienates people from poetry since poetry can be so personal, just as a song can be personal. What appeals to one person is rarely what appeals to another.

A Poetry Table is an equalizing experience. I'm a human. You're a human. You may be my boss, but you are not my superior in any way during a Poetry Table. There is no hierarchy. We are all on the same level as humans. When gathered around a Poetry Table, team members are truly equal.

Similarly, doing a Poetry Table may, for many people, be a new way of experiencing poetry, a fresh encounter. In the small groups, I want people to interact in a different way; drop their masks; say something innocent, naïve, foolish, unfiltered, imperfect; show emotion; and reveal something about themselves. These aren't rules or expectations. They are hopes. The idea is to set up a safe environment where these things might happen.

A direct approach would not work for most people. If I asked people some of the questions directly, without the poem as a vehicle, as a catalyst for conversation and self-disclosure, most people would not open up. What matters to you? What is your purpose? What is your passion? These questions are too direct. People would be uncomfortable. They might not know what to say. Indirect approaches often work better, especially at first when people are "feeling things out." The poem speaks for them, and they align with it. It gives them a voice.

Reading poetry and talking about it are intimate acts, opening you up to your deepest concerns, loves, feelings. A poem can activate your secret life. This secret life could be forgotten, dormant, smoldering, unknown, hidden, or repressed. Reading a poem and talking about it can be an awakening, a reawakening, or a realization. Thoughts like the following often arise: "Oh yes, this is important to me. I had forgotten how important this is to me. I need to take action. I can't keep waiting. I can't keep putting it off."

CHAPTER 5

Background

I LOVED FREIGHT TRAINS when I was a kid—really, really loved them. The noise, the motion, and the engines' power deeply appealed to me. From an early age, whenever I could, I would go to my grandparents' house at the edge of the small country town of Giddings, Texas. It was my childhood paradise.

About 100 yards behind their home was a Southern Pacific railroad track. I loved the rumble of the diesel motors, the honking of the horn, and the variety of names and places on the boxcars: Erie and Lackawanna, Cotton Belt, Chesapeake and Ohio, Norfolk and Western. I liked the words, the sounds of the words. The names of faraway places sparked my imagination. I used to look up the names in my encyclopedia to learn more. Lackawanna! Where is that? I was intrigued by saying the words and thinking about their origins. Seeing the names on those train cars ignited an interest in language and what it represented.

While I was interested in language, I didn't come to poetry until my mid-thirties. I don't recall reading poetry as a kid or anything about poetry from English classes in high school or college. No good or bad experiences. No poems. Nothing. No memories of poetry at all. The only poetic language I recall from childhood was from the King James version of the Bible. I grew up going to a Lutheran church and heard scripture from the Old Testament on a regular basis.

I don't recall any exposure to poetry until my mid to late twenties when, after a period of depression, I was trying to find my way through my lostness. I took a poetry writing class at the University of Houston, which had one of the best creative writing programs in the United States at the time. The class was great, and excruciating. I wasn't ready for the intimacy and intensity of poetry. I was too terrified to write much, but I felt something stirring. I was taking baby steps in the direction of poetry and deep feeling. There was something about poetry that attracted and scared me. Writing poetry made me feel uncomfortable and vulnerable, which I disliked. And so, I set poetry aside for a few more years until I took a poetry workshop in 1994 with the poet Arthur Sze in Santa Fe, New Mexico, where I had moved in 1992. I don't recall why I took Arthur's workshop, but this time, the timing was right. I was hooked.

With Arthur's encouragement, I decided to immerse myself in poetry and pursue a degree in writing. I chose the low-residency Master of Fine Arts in Poetry program at Vermont College. I specifically recall doing it for the love of poetry, for the joy of it. I felt a deep, energetic connection to poetry, a coming home, which felt honest, authentic, and true. I wanted to set aside time to study poetry in depth.

Pursuing a degree wasn't a practical decision. I didn't need it for a job. The decision didn't have to do with making more money. In fact, I felt liberated that a poetry degree was so outside of the American economy, the American financial system, so financially worthless. The moment felt unique in my life.

One major thread for the Poetry Table concept goes back to my experience as a ninth grade English teacher at Milby High School, an inner-city school in Houston. I had students who didn't read books on their own, so I instituted a reading and writing workshop.

I didn't pick the books for the students. I couldn't know what they would like and relate to. Choice was key. Books were made accessible. They had to read for a set number of minutes in class. At first, the time allotted was short. As they became comfortable reading, I increased the length of time. Then, they wrote in their journals. At first, the assignment was freewriting. They could write whatever they wanted for a fixed time. Gradually, I increased the writing time. Sometimes I had questions for them to answer.

The successes were enormous. Some students were slow readers and read only a few books. Others read quickly and read many books. Over the school year, one student read over thirty books. Another took her books home. Her mother called to let me know her daughter was reading at home and how grateful she was. She never used to do so, her mother told me, but now she was reading all the time. As a teacher, that was (and still is) a gratifying and rewarding comment.

I did have guidelines that the book had to be a storybook, not a picture book. It couldn't be a how-to manual. The book had to have characters or real people in it. It could be fiction or non-fiction. Besides encouraging students to read, my other goals were to create empathy, to help students understand people who were different, to encourage them to travel imaginatively, to enter other worlds, even if they picked books with worlds that seemed similar to their own.

The Poetry Table is, in many ways, a continuation of those reading and writing workshops. I am bringing poems to people who probably don't read poetry. The purpose of a Poetry Table isn't to turn people into poetry readers. If they decide to read poetry after the experience, then so much the better. The purpose is to give them a personal, powerful, reflective experience of poetry, and for them to learn something surprising about themselves and others.

Another influential experience is worth mentioning, and it has impacted how I facilitate. It didn't include poetry, but it did include the powerful questions, small groups, deep connection, and personal storytelling that are so instrumental in the design of Poetry Tables.

In 1996, I worked at the Institute for Intercultural Leadership (IICL) at Santa Fe Community College. IICL was asked by the City of Santa Fe to structure a facilitation process to help the city deal with a complicated and contentious community issue. During World War II, there had been a Japanese internment camp in Santa Fe. In 1996, the aging internees and their descendants wanted the Santa Fe government to install a large memorial at the site. The size of the proposed memorial and the word "memorial" triggered opposition. Veterans' groups angrily challenged the initiative.

My colleagues at IICL proposed a simple but powerful facilitation process. Small, balanced groups of veterans and their supporters were mixed with internees and their supporters. The small groups created intimacy. The small-group guidelines encouraged people to listen to understand, be curious, contribute, and participate. Each group had a facilitator to guide the process and ask questions. The questions were simple, personal, and constructed so people could tell their stories. For example, why is it important for you to be here today? What is at the heart of the matter for you? The initial questions weren't about solving anything. The purpose of the initial conversations was to permit people to speak from the heart, build trust, and connect people to others' humanity.

The outcome was astounding. The initial emotional charge dissipated and transformed as people became genuine and real. Grief poured out. Many of the veterans were Bataan Death March survivors. They didn't have a memorial. Their sacrifice hadn't been honored with a public structure.

As the process evolved, win-win solutions emerged. A consensus developed that instead of a memorial, the City of Santa Fe would place a historical marker at the internment camp site. The City of Santa Fe would build a monument to honor the veterans. In addition to the public structures, there were transformations: changes in people's affect, shifts between people, reconciliations. The social fabric in the community grew stronger as people connected and bridged divides.

To this day, I am moved by talking about the experience, which convinced me that the most contentious issues can be overcome if the people at odds can connect deeply, humanly first.

A DIVIDED LIFE

Although I spent the time, energy, and money to get a Master of Fine Arts in Poetry degree, I kept poetry and my work life separated. People I worked with didn't know about my poetry life: the graduate degree, the poetry groups I was in, and that I wrote poetry early in the morning before work.

In 2005, feeling stuck professionally, I decided to get a Master of Science in Organization Development degree from Pepperdine University. A year and a half into the program, in January 2007, the writer and consultant Peter Block came to Laguna, California, to work with the cohort of thirty-one adult students. During an evening fireside chat, Peter suggested that instead of talking about organizational development, we sing, read poetry, or do something artistic or creative. Peter asked the class, "Who has a poem?" I blurted out, "I do." Peter said, "Well, then read it." I read the following poem, which I had with me because I had already decided it was time to share a hidden part of myself with my classmates.

To the Animal Not Roadkill

For the poodle in Corpus Christi,
I feel awful, still.

And for the gliding roadrunner
outside Santa Fe, my regret has not ebbed.

* * * * * *
You survived
by a hair, a nose, a foot, for what it matters—a mile.

Because I bought organic half & half and veggie meatloaf.
Not because I bought them.

Because I took my own plastic bags, recycle.
Not.

If I had braked.
Because I braked.

Because at a propitious moment in history
I swerved.

Because of El Nino, La Nina,
a ripple from another famine in Africa.

If the Moon had been in Leo . . .
If that night had no moon.

Your death couldn't have been closer, and more likely.
I toast your health, continued good fortune.

Now knowing
you've received the ultimate reprieve

how will you live?

    David Markwardt

After I finished reading, out of the silence one of my classmates looked at me and said, "You are like a whole other person!"

I was stunned. It was a wake-up call for me. To this day, so many years later, I still see her look and feel the shock of her comment. I had been appearing one way to my classmates. Part of me was missing, a big part. I was living a divided life, which was costing me and, ultimately, costing them. I wasn't bringing my full self to them, my gifts and talents, the things I care about. I had separated soul and role. My work role was as a facilitator, team builder, leadership trainer. My soul was connected to poetry. In the years since, I have explored integrating poetry into my work. Poetry Tables are a manifestation of my exploration.

Perhaps you can relate to my story. Perhaps you are living a divided life and are not being true to yourself. A purpose of Poetry Tables is the possibility of redemption and making you more whole.

"Let the beauty of what you love be what you do."

Rumi

CHAPTER 6

Gradient

The Way It Is

There's a thread you follow. It goes among
things that change. But it doesn't change.
People wonder about what you are pursuing.
You have to explain about the thread.
But it is hard for others to see.
While you hold it you can't get lost.
Tragedies happen; people get hurt
or die; and you suffer and get old.
Nothing you do can stop time's unfolding.
You don't ever let go of the thread.

William Stafford

A THREAD IS CONTINUOUS and runs through your life. The thread is tied to your individuality. It is distinctive as your fingerprints. Each individual has their own thread, which doesn't change because it connects to your uniqueness. In the previous chapter, I mentioned threads in my life that merged into Poetry Tables.

"It is hard for others to see." Other people have their threads and have a hard time seeing your thing, your thread. A big part of your life journey is seeing and believing in your thread, accepting it, having faith in its uniqueness and your singular voice, your gifts, and communicating your thread so others can see it.

The line "While you hold it you can't get lost" reminds me of Carl Jung's term *gradient,* introduced to me by the mythologist and storyteller Michael Meade. In the mid-1990s, I saw Meade in Santa Fe, New Mexico. He talked about being close to your gradient, your soul, your true self. He demonstrated this by pretending that there was a center line on the stage floor. When you are away from your gradient, then you are lost. He moved away from the line. When you are close to the line, you are found. He moved closer to the line. You are close to your life's energy. Things flow for you when you are close to your gradient.

Since then, I've read more about what Jung meant by the gradient. Jung believed everyone is born with one and has it throughout their life. The key is to stay close to it, though this can be challenging.

Jung felt that your energy's flow had a definite direction—a natural, right way. If you could follow it, then you could realize the Self. "No other way is like yours. All other ways deceive and tempt you. You must fulfill the way that is in you."[2] Yet, following your natural gradient (way) is difficult and made more difficult by the larger culture, which is not interested in your self-actualization. It would prefer you go its way, buy its products, consume and consume, pursue its vision of success, and live your life in socially acceptable ways. If the culture is aligned with your gradient, then you are in luck, but if not, then you face struggle, choices, and risks.

Such devilish bargains never turn out well for the Self. Perhaps you are living a divided life as I was. Perhaps years pass imperceptibly, and the energy of your life atrophies. Your aliveness wanes, and you don't

---

2. C.G. Jung, *The Red Book* (New York: W.W. Norton & Company, 2009), 308.

even notice it is gone or take it seriously until you have a severe bout of depression, a divorce, or a midlife crisis.

A Poetry Table is a reflective experience, a reflective moment, which can take you back to your gradient. The experience can access your deep inner life and touch your soul. Wislawa Szymborska puts forth the notion that the soul is something that comes and goes. You can't force it to show up. You can be attentive for it to appear. The paradox is that expecting it can hinder its attendance. A Poetry Table helps us to coax the soul to come forth.

A Few Words on the Soul

We have a soul at times.
No one's got it non-stop,
for keeps.

Day after day,
year after year
may pass without it.

Sometimes
it will settle for awhile
only in childhood's fears and raptures.
Sometimes only in astonishment
that we are old.

It rarely lends a hand
in uphill tasks,
like moving furniture,
or lifting luggage,
or going miles in shoes that pinch.

It usually steps out
whenever meat needs chopping
or forms have to be filled.

For every thousand conversations

it participates in one,
if even that,
since it prefers silence.

Just when our body goes from ache to pain,
it slips off-duty.

It's picky:
it doesn't like seeing us in crowds,
our hustling for a dubious advantage
and creaky machinations make it sick.

Joy and sorrow
aren't two different feelings for it.
It attends us
only when the two are joined.

We can count on it
when we're sure of nothing
and curious about everything.

Among the material objects
it favors clocks with pendulums
and mirrors, which keep on working
even when no one is looking.

It won't say where it comes from
or when it's taking off again,
though it's clearly expecting such questions.

We need it
but apparently
it needs us
for some reason too.

    Wislawa Szymborska

The soul may surface during the silence of reading poems during a
Poetry Table. Ripe conditions may be silence and unexpectedness. If you

immerse yourself in the experience and let down your guard, then the deeper self may emerge. But if you know a Poetry Table is planned and approach the experience with the expectation your soul will show up, then it may not. It probably won't. Life—your soul—may not comply.

When I was in high school playing basketball and had a good first half, scoring more than anyone else, I sometimes got ahead of myself and started thinking about the second half and the pure glory of scoring even more. But more often than not, I didn't come close. As soon as I became self-conscious, dreaming about the second half, I got out of the flow and rhythm. If people come to a Poetry Table with the expectation they are going to go deep, have an epiphany, an incredible insight, and deeply connect with their peers, they may be disappointed. There could be a gap between their expectations and their experience. If they come without expectations and are open, bold, courageous, vulnerable, willing to take risks and contribute, then something different is more likely to happen. They may see the thing they hope to see or something else, perhaps even better, out of the corner of their eye.

I am reminded of a poem about being attentive and mindful by Czeslaw Milosz, which he wrote while he lived in Berkeley, California.

Gift

A day so happy.
Fog lifted early, I worked in the garden.
Hummingbirds were stopping over honeysuckle flowers.
There was no thing on earth I wanted to possess.
I knew no one worth my envying him.
Whatever evil I had suffered, I forgot.
To think that once I was the same man did not embarrass me.
In my body I felt no pain.
When straightening up, I saw the blue sea and sails.

Czeslaw Milosz

The "right" state of showing up is about intention and readiness. Much of life seems this way. When I don't expect to see the wild animal is when I see it. Ideally, I am present, attentive. I can't be on my phone, thinking about other things, far away things, envy, desire, regrets, worry, the past, or the future. As Mark Twain wrote, "I've had many troubles in my life, most of which never happened."

CHAPTER 7

Connect People

*"Stranger, if you passing meet me and desire to speak to me, why should
you not speak to me? And why should I not speak to you?"*

Walt Whitman

A POETRY TABLE CONNECTS strangers and friends even if they think
they know each other well. I can think of groups of people who have
worked together for many years and "know" each other. A Poetry
Table is a way to open a new conversation, one we haven't had no
matter how long we have known each other, whether we are old friends
or strangers. It is a potent team and community-building activity.
Reading poems and discussing them in a personal way and in a small
group can open doors to accelerating trust and revitalizing or deepening relationships.

This can happen with any level of relationship and at any age. It
doesn't matter how different people are. There could be differences
in gender, race, religion, or even deeper differences in personality
or temperament. Sharing a poem and talking about how it relates
to your life can cut through all of that. A Poetry Table expands the

boundaries of our being and gives us a sense of the interconnectedness with all living things. As Poet Walt Whitman said, "We contain multitudes."

Our current focus on identity is increasingly reductive. Poetry Tables, on the other hand, are expansive. For anyone committed to a lifetime of growth, curiosity, and learning, a Poetry Table can be done endlessly. For three years, I facilitated the annual retreat for a city attorney and her diverse team. Every year she wanted to do a Poetry Table at the retreat. Every year participants picked a different poem and shared something new about themselves.

The Pulitzer Prize–winning writer, Annie Dillard, said:

"In the deeps are the violence and terror of which psychology has warned us. But if you ride these monsters deeper down, if you drop with them farther over the world's rim, you find what our sciences cannot locate or name, the substrate, the ocean or matrix or ether which buoys the rest, which gives goodness its power for good, and evil its power for evil, the unified field: our complex and inexplicable caring for each other, and for our life together here. This is given. It is not learned."[3]

This is the purpose, partly, of a Poetry Table, to create an experience where people can come to a place beyond their monsters, dragons, fears, and vulnerabilities, and arrive at a place of "our complex and inexplicable caring for each other, and for our life together here." In daily life, it is hard to stay in this connected place. It may be enough to have a glimpse of a larger, more interconnected world.

One of my favorite poems by Czeslaw Milosz is one of his last.

---

3. Annie Dillard, *Teaching a Stone to Talk: Expeditions and Encounters* (New York: Harper Perennial, 2013).

Late Ripeness

Not soon, as late as the approach of my ninetieth year,
I felt a door opening in me and I entered
the clarity of early morning.

One after another my former lives were departing,
like ships, together with their sorrow.

And the countries, cities, gardens, the bays of seas
assigned to my brush came closer,
ready now to be described better than they were before.

I was not separated from people,
grief and pity joined us.
We forget—I kept saying—that we are all children of
the King.

For where we come from there is no division
into Yes and No, into is, was, and will be.

We were miserable, we used no more than a hundredth part
of the gift we received for our long journey.

Moments from yesterday and from centuries ago—
a sword blow, the painting of eyelashes before a mirror
of polished metal, a lethal musket shot, a caravel
staving its hull against a reef—they dwell in us,
waiting for a fulfillment.

I knew, always, that I would be a worker in the vineyard,
as are all men and women living at the same time,
whether they are aware of it or not.

Czeslaw Milosz

I love this poem and could talk about it at length, perhaps even
write a whole book about it. For now, I'll focus on the first stanza. What

draws me to the poem is the message that our journey and spiritual growth isn't over until we die. Milosz was approaching ninety!

Regardless of age, a person can learn, ripen, have insights, renewal, and rebirth; they can feel a door opening and enter the clarity of early morning. For many people, reading poetry provides clarity. People see what they need to do, know where they need to go, bright and clear like early morning after a good night's sleep, before the day's intrusions and life's noise and deceptions muddy the picture.

Another part of the poem that draws me to it are the lines about our commonalities. The experience of a Poetry Table can break down separations between people.

> I was not separated from people,
> grief and pity joined us.
> We forget—I kept saying—that we are all children of
> the King.
>
> For where we come from there is no division
> into Yes and No, into is, was, and will be

Relating the poem to your life and speaking openly about it bridges divisions. The things that divide us—politics, gender, race, nationality, hierarchies, and class—may seem important, but maybe they are not. At the end, we are all human and "children of the King"—of God. "From where we come from," we are born without the divisions and then living in the world imposes them on us. People often share how they experience their commonalities with others from doing a Poetry Table together.

A Poetry Table is a way to connect and respect people so it is easier to see commonalities and to say we are all humans or global citizens. We can then take collective action towards life's challenges.

Here is another poem about shared humanity.

Hook

I was only a young man
In those days. On that evening
The cold was so God damned
Bitter there was nothing.
Nothing. I was in trouble
With a woman, and there was nothing
There but me and dead snow.

I stood on the street corner
In Minneapolis, lashed
This way and that.
Wind rose from some pit,
Hunting me.
Another bus to Saint Paul
Would arrive in three hours,
If I was lucky.

Then the young Sioux
Loomed beside me, his scars
Were just my age.

Ain't got no bus here
A long time, he said.
You got enough money
To get home on?

What did they do
To your hand? I answered.
He raised up his hook into the terrible starlight
And slashed the wind.

Oh, that? he said.
I had a bad time with a woman. Here,
You take this.

Did you ever feel a man hold
Sixty-five cents

In a hook,
And place it
Gently
In your freezing hand?

I took it.
It wasn't the money I needed.
But I took it.

James Wright

"Hook" matters to me because it explores a moment of connecting on a deep human level with a stranger. For me, it is a poem about overcoming isolation, about generosity, giving, and about receiving. It may be about overcoming differences of race and background. The poem sounds autobiographical, like it is from James Wright's personal experience, though we don't know for sure since it is a poem, a work of art. I could see it having many uses, including diversity training and for leadership and management programs.

Below is one of my poems about connection.

White Hearse

When the white hearse passed
a thousand mouths closed
at the chili cook-off.

Beer rippled to a standstill in plastic cups.
Spoons rested in peace
in bowls of ground beef and beans.

People rose in respect.
Baseball caps came off
in the town square.

One could hear a crow squawk

at the top of a live oak.

I stared out in wonder
at solemn faces of random strangers.

The steel of our automobile
did not separate us.

Joined, for a time
from where we came from
and where we are going, people stood
until the last car of the procession
passed by.

David Markwardt

I wrote "White Hearse" in 2014 after my Aunt Tiny's funeral in Round Top, Texas. She was my father's brother's wife and the last close family member of my father's generation to die. When I was growing up in the 1960s, Round Top was a German immigrant farming community. By 2014, it had lost much of its immigrant character, but the rural response to the funeral procession showed it maintained a traditional respect toward life and death.

I recall a bank manager from Espanola, New Mexico, picking "White Hearse" in a leadership program. She was Hispanic and could trace her ancestors back to the conquistadors. Espanola is a traditional northern New Mexico community, with long-standing customs. What drew her to the poem was the title, the opening stanza, and how the celebration was interrupted. The words, lines, and images that stood out for her were "the white hearse," "a thousand mouths closed" and "chili cook-off." It was a vivid scene she said. She was also drawn to the images of partying and celebration—"beer rippled to a standstill in plastic cups" followed by "people rose in respect./ Baseball caps came off/in the town square."

She said that in her community, people too often have feuds about trivial matters, sometimes lasting for years, even generations, but then set them aside and come together over tragedy. She connected with the poem across distance, time, and culture. She could relate to people putting aside petty differences to focus on what matters. People could be at odds with each other and then, poof, could set it aside for a funeral. Likewise, this is what a Poetry Table helps us to do.

CHAPTER 8

Educare and the Experiential Learning Cycle

THE LATIN WORD *EDUCARE* means "to draw out." It is a complementary term to gradient. Education is often pouring information, content, or data into a person, filling someone up from the outside in, giving them knowledge. In contrast, *educare* means educating from the inside out, drawing upon the student's nature and experience to connect to the world around them.

Both outside-in and inside-out approaches have value and validity. If you're going to be a doctor, you benefit, obviously, from extensive training, from much "pouring in" of medical knowledge. You are told the names of the muscles, how they function, how they can be damaged and repaired.

As a patient, I want my doctor to be an expert in their specialty. I want my doctor to know the most current medical and scientific research and practices, as I would with any professional. I also want the best, most knowledgeable, technically skilled plumber around. Informational competency and knowledge go far, but only so far in developing a good doctor. The ability to connect, to relate, to respond to and acknowledge feelings, and the internal qualities and interpersonal skills of the professional matter a great deal, and may matter more than technical competency. At times, a patient needs a caring, emotionally intelligent human as much as or more than a technically competent, logical professional.

A Poetry Table operates in a context. There is an element of outside-in to Poetry Tables in the structuring and tone setting of the tables, the provision of the poems, and the guiding questions. Nevertheless, a Poetry Table is more an inside-out activity.

Poetry is the means by which you draw insights forth from yourself. The experience is not about gaining competence and knowledge about poetry, though a Poetry Table could be used to teach poetry as well as draw out personal meaning.

In a Poetry Table, we redefine what "help" means. The role of a good educator, therapist, facilitator, or leader isn't to advise. In the spirit of *educare*, helping means to support you to discover, nurture emergence, and encourage you to find the self-courage to see something and take action. From this perspective, you already have embedded within you all the tools you need to make yourself whole. In other words, helping and educating is not trying to save by giving advice but is providing a profound experience and asking compelling, powerful questions so you find your own internal wisdom and courage to act.

When I was training to become a National Outdoor Leadership School (NOLS) instructor, I remember hearing the term *educare* during the NOLS instructor's course. The NOLS course training was both inside out and outside in, giving me the technical skills to become competent in the wilderness while drawing out qualities inside me to use them wisely. Two people with comparable wilderness skills might be very different instructors because of their internal qualities. One could be an excellent instructor, the other not as good. The excellent instructor would have mastered "hard" technical skills and "soft" human, interpersonal, and emotional intelligence skills.

The two sets of skills are misnamed. The hardest skills to master are the "soft" skills. They generally require a lifetime of learning and internal transformational change. To be kind, courageous, and compassionate are internal qualities. One is never done learning and mastering them.

Experiential training typically includes a large *educare* element. For example, challenge courses (ropes courses) with high events are not about making people more competent at tackling challenge courses or climbing. They are, instead, a means to an end and a metaphor. They are a catalyst for conversation, first with the self, and then with others. At their best, challenge courses provide a powerful, memorable experience that awakens people to competencies and strengths they didn't know they had, that shake them up. A challenge course may help you see others and yourself in a new way. You may overcome limiting belief systems and find the internal strength to do something despite your fear. The experience is followed by questions that ask you to reflect upon its lessons.

The classic experiential learning cycle invented by David Kolb[4] is to have an experience, reflect upon it (usually encouraged and supported by a facilitator, coach, or teacher who asks questions), conceptualize how you might apply the lessons learned to your life, and then experiment, do something new.

Poetry Tables have much in common with experiential education exercises. Ropes courses, indoor problem-solving activities, wilderness trips, and poetry all have the power to change lives through direct experience. All are learning-by-doing exercises, or, at least, learning by experiencing. None are easy to understand in advance. You have to do them, experience them, to access the learning.

---

4. D. A. Kolb, *Experiential learning: Experience as the source of learning and development (Vol. 1)* (Englewood Cliffs, NJ: Prentice-Hall, 1984).

The Experiential Learning Cycle

In addition, I have hosted Poetry Tables several times in outdoor settings. I have facilitated them in national parks on picnic tables under ponderosa pines and in gardens, parks, and labyrinths. These natural settings are great places for Poetry Tables. They add to the spiritual experience. Although I am comfortable with traditional classroom learning and teaching knowledge, facts, and information, I am also very comfortable offering the space so people can have visceral learning experiences. They all open up a part of the brain that inspires wonder and awe.

In the spirit of *educare,* a Poetry Table is not about determining an objective meaning for the poems. We don't talk about a poem's meter or analyze what it means. A Poetry Table is not an analytical academic exercise. It is a reflective thinking-and-feeling exercise. It is a heartfelt exercise. A Poetry Table is about finding a deep, meaningful personal relationship with a poem while others in the small group find theirs and developing a deeper connection with self and others through self-disclosure.

Poet Billy Collins addresses the typical obsession with objective meaning in his poem "Introduction to Poetry."

Introduction to Poetry

I ask them to take a poem
and hold it up to the light
like a color slide

or press an ear against its hive.

I say drop a mouse into a poem
and watch him probe his way out,

or walk inside the poem's room
and feel the walls for a light switch.

I want them to waterski
across the surface of a poem
waving at the author's name on the shore.

But all they want to do
is tie the poem to a chair with rope
and torture a confession out of it.

They begin beating it with a hose
to find out what it really means.

Billy Collins

What draws me to this poem is its wit and the balance between playfulness and curiosity. I like the idea that poetry is something to be experienced and explored from different perspectives and angles, for readers to be patient, have fun, and be inquisitive with a poem.

MESSAGE IN A BOTTLE

A poet wants to say something about the present that extends into the future. A poem wants to last beyond the immediate moment. A poem tries to overcome distance, in all its aspects: physical distance and time. A metaphor sometimes used for poems is that each is a message in a bottle. The poet rolls up the poem, puts it in a bottle, corks it, and tosses it into the sea. When and where it washes up, and who finds and reads it, is a mystery.

The message in a bottle is a beautiful image. The finder finds the gift from afar, from another time and place, from a stranger they will never meet. It's possible the bottle will never be found. But when it is found, that discovery can be a miracle.

The experiential stories I shared earlier felt true and miraculous to the people who found their poems. A distinction needs to be made; the stories aren't what felt true and miraculous—the experience did. The stories were about the experiences. That is what a Poetry Table does when it hits the mark. A participant finds a poem that rings shockingly and surprisingly true to some part of their experience. It strikes. It comes out of the dark like a lightning bolt.

They may not have the language to describe what they are experiencing. They may not be aware of it until they read the poem. In the best cases, that possibility of giving voice to another's inner life isn't just open to the poet's contemporaries. It may live on past the poet's life.

Anne Sexton was dead when the construction manager, Charlie, read "Courage." Her poem outlived her. It spoke directly to a man who didn't know her, might not have even liked her if they met, and probably wouldn't have crossed paths with her even if they were alive at the same time. How would they have met? What did they have in common anyway? Charlie was a construction manager in Texas. She was a poet in Massachusetts. And yet, she wrote a poem that touched him. She expressed something in "Courage" about grief and healing that he hadn't heard expressed in any other way. She spoke for his grief and his healing. Her words moved him and moved him forward, which is what healing is—forward movement. Meaningful poetry can do this, as can any profound literature and art. It can speak to different peoples and generations, and cross boundaries of time, nationality, and religion.

CHAPTER 9

Storytelling

"Poetry is the story of the human heart."

Billy Collins

TALKING ABOUT THE POEM, telling why it matters to you and how it intersects with your work and life during a Poetry Table, is a powerful form of storytelling. Telling your story in this manner is almost always a surefire way to connect with and engage others. The poem is a catalyst for deep connection, conversation, and meaning-making.

Storytelling in poetry can take many forms. Many poems contain a story or hint of a story. "Hook" and "White Hearse" are examples. Other poems are thematically arranged. "A Few Words on the Soul" is an example. A story in a poem is a powerful way for readers to relate to it. Below is an example that I use in almost every Poetry Table across generations.

Autobiography in Five Short Chapters

Chapter One
I walk down the street.
There is a deep hole in the sidewalk.
I fall in.
I am lost…I am helpless.
It isn't my fault.
It takes forever to find a way out.

Chapter Two
I walk down the same street.
There is a deep hole in the sidewalk.
I pretend I don't see it.
I fall in again.
I can't believe I am in this same place.
But, it isn't my fault.
It still takes a long time to get out.

Chapter Three
I walk down the same street.
There is a deep hole in the sidewalk.
I see it is there.
I still fall in… it's a habit . . . but,
my eyes are open.
I know where I am.
It is my fault.
I get out immediately.

Chapter Four
I walk down the same street.
There is a deep hole in the sidewalk.
I walk around it.

Chapter Five
I walk down another street.

Portia Nelson

I can think of so many people who picked this poem and then told stories of being blind, or caught in cyclical loops of destructive behavior, or in unhealthy ruts and then escaping them. The human dilemma described in the poem is a common one. Most people can relate to being in a damaging pattern at some point in their life, when their thinking doesn't work, because rather than genuine thought, it's habit of thought, a bad habit, a blinding belief system, or a knee-jerk reaction to circumstances.

Whether a poem has a story in it or not, you tell your story when you talk about the poem. Why does the poem matter to you? Why did you pick it? How does the poem intersect with your life and work? Anyone who honestly answers the last question will tell part of their story.

CHAPTER 10

Naming

"After great pain, a formal feeling comes."

Emily Dickinson

POET JAY PARINI SAID, "Anyone can understand this feeling, which is a need as well. When a loved one dies, for example, a funeral or memorial service follows: a formal event that mirrors the urge toward form that comes in the wake of tragedy. The ceremony is useful in helping those in grief to assuage their feelings, to organize their thoughts and recollections, to imagine themselves in relation to the loss that has caused the pain. There is something about the ceremony itself that assists in making the pain endurable by, in obvious ways, naming it. Without the ceremony, those in grief would experience a mess of unnamed, even unrecognized, feelings."

A huge part of poetry's value is recognizing and naming pain and loss and, possibly, providing healing. For the engineer whose son died from suicide, the poem he picked, "Kindness," was naming and healing. For the construction manager who lost his daughter in a car accident, the poem he picked, "Courage," provided the same.

I am sure they had funerals after their children died. Those funerals may have been healing. However, they were not enough, since moving through grief can be a lifelong process. Something else was necessary. Both men found additional healing sometime later through the distilled language and compact form of a poem.

I have experienced this need myself and wrote the following poem for my father's funeral in 2000.

Accounting

He can figure percentages in a flash:
exact, errorless, without a calculator.
I can too, without wanting,
without trying.
One afternoon in late September
showing my tax return
my father's old math-mind-magic returns;
he leans toward the numbers.
Some men lean together
in beer-stained armchairs toward games
on Sunday afternoons, the TV commentators
doing the talking, others against rifles
in drafty deer blinds. At times we had leaned
those ways, but accounting is closer
to home. He spots a charitable donation
I haven't claimed. Talking taxes
is not what I wanted as a young man.
I pushed him to lean
as the winds of my requests shifted.
He pushed back. I moved away
not calling to endure
gaps of silence on the phone
until I found my way as he found
when, leaving his father's farm,
he opened his accounting firm.

Anger drained, I met him where he was
and now, taking a break from Schedule A
we walk outside on a brilliant New Mexico day,
admiring over a thousand tomatoes in my garden.
You've got a green thumb
like my father had, he says with a bounce.
We stand together in silence
watching fruit ripening.
My wife joins us.
Rubbing her belly, I feel the boy inside
kick toward my hand
or, I wonder, is he pushing
and I think I understand: my father pushed
like his father pushed
and my son will push, and I
pray before the final accounting
we will lean together.

David Markwardt

Writing the poem and then reading it at the funeral provided additional closure for me.

Hearing the poem also provided additional closure for many people attending. Twenty-one years later, at my mother's funeral, I spoke to a cousin who recalled me reading "Accounting." It had stuck with her.

A poem can articulate something a reader can't quite say and hasn't found the words for. Much of our lives can seem chaotic, disorderly, fragmented. A poem can give us order and wholeness, even if it is transitory. A poem has a form, a shape. The words are ordered and arranged in a certain way. Poet Robert Frost said that poetry offers a "momentary stay against confusion." Frost is correct. We vacillate between clarity and confusion. The little poetic forms, made of intentionally arranged words, "messages in a bottle," in "Kindness," "Courage," and "Don't Quit" helped the readers name their experiences, provided a moment of clarity, and were steps for each of them in understanding their lives and in healing.

The poem is the vehicle to the emotions. It is an intermediary to the inner life and evokes the revelation. There is something amazing about the language and form of a poem that triggers insight and epiphany. A poem's words, lines, and images can offer something mysterious and unique, even sacred.

CHAPTER 11

The Importance of Metaphor

"The material comforts brought forth by abundance ultimately matter
much less than the metaphors you live by—whether, say,
you think of your life as a journey or as a treadmill.
A large part of self-understanding is the search for
appropriate personal metaphors that make sense of our lives."

George Lakoff, *Metaphors We Live By*

METAPHOR IS AN ESSENTIAL form of thought. Metaphor is commonly defined as a figure of speech in which a word or phrase is applied to an object or action to which it is not literally applicable. It may provide clarity or identify hidden similarities between two ideas. The more we understand metaphor, the better we understand ourselves.

In poetry, metaphor is more expansive than the above definition suggests. In poetry, "metaphor is about comparison, and it engenders a sense of connection and kindness," poet Miriam Sagan said. Think about the difference between the words *journey* and *treadmill*. In a journey, forward movement leads somewhere to and beyond a changing horizon; on a treadmill, forward movement is illusory—you are expending effort, but do not gain ground; instead, you go over the same ground again and again.

Additionally, sounds of words matter. Sometimes, they echo meaning. The vowels and consonants of journey sound softer and forgiving. There's a longer time element, a bigger context of seeing individual things and events on a journey. If "bad" things—regrets, mistakes—happen on your journey, then they are part of the learning, stepping stones. Treadmill sounds harder and connotes rat race. It sounds unforgiving as a metaphor. There's a harshness to it.

A metaphor you could use to think about your life journey is a stream.

The Stream

There is a stream you were born in.
You didn't know you were in it. You sang,
rhymed wild sounds, drew pictures
of a grinning boy with flames shooting from his hair.
Then over the slow accumulation of days
people tugged at you, fished you out
into unfamiliar streams, their murky waters.
At first you fought. But their tackle
was too powerful, led to slow deadening.
You didn't even know you were out, or when.
Still you survived. Got older. Matured.
Memory of your stream tugs at you, an adult.
Always there, a stream is yours.
Always buoyant, it will bear you up.
No one can dam it any more,
except you. Listen to its good voice
as it rushes over rocks.

David Markwardt

When I worked on ropes courses, I used the events as a type of metaphor. The ropes course, especially high events, pushed people out of their comfort zones. That tension, the fear, was good and helpful for people to think creatively and metaphorically. Some fear and discomfort were good for learning. It forced people to reckon with their feelings in an immediate way. It stimulated aliveness. It was not good or helpful if the discomfort was overwhelming. Learning couldn't happen if people were in the panic zone.

Similar principles apply with a Poetry Table. Reading poetry and talking about it can get people out of their comfort zone, sometimes way out. That tension, the discomfort, the vulnerability, is good. It gets the blood moving and helps people think creatively, expansively, and metaphorically. At the same time, the leap can't be too soon or so great that people panic, shut down, and can't see the connections and relationships, and imagine possibilities.

Robert Frost suggested that a person uneducated in the operations of metaphor was not safe in the world, should not even be let out of doors. This ability to connect the dots, to see relationships between seemingly disparate things, and recognize continuity and connections between different events in your life, are essential to meaning-making and figuring out your journey.

You can get stuck in the repetitive patterns of the language you use and in your assumptions. You can use language without examining it, without being conscious of alternative ways of expressing what you are experiencing, like being on a treadmill. The fresh language in a poem may get you out of this rut, open you to a new way of thinking and seeing, and offer a different perspective. The metaphors, similes, and analogies in poems can help readers see new paths and possibilities for their lives.

In many ways, both individually and collectively, one key to confronting and transforming our most intractable problems is to imagine a new metaphor for a situation. If we can think about a conflict in a new way, with fresh language and a fresh metaphor representing fresh thinking, then we may be on our way to seeing new possibilities.

CHAPTER 12

Delightfully Surprised

PEOPLE, INCLUDING ME, ARE delightfully surprised during Poetry Tables. As a facilitator of numerous workshops, I find many activities can be predictable after a while. Not so with Poetry Tables. They are always fresh for me as a facilitator. Part of the reward and delight is seeing which poems people choose and what they have to say about them. They are never predictable.

You, the participant-reader, are reintroduced to poetry in a surprisingly positive way, perhaps more than when you were in high school. Maybe you just come from a place of curiosity and are interested to learn. Or maybe life isn't turning out the way you want. Maybe you have had setbacks, losses in family or work. Illusions and delusions may have distorted your life. Maybe it's time to be honest with yourself: "Who am I?" "What am I here to do?" "What is my purpose?" "What gives me meaning?" "Is the money I'm making and the life I am living worth it?" "Are the sacrifices worth it?" "Is my life too practical?" "Am I doing what is in my heart?" "How long will I keep putting *it* off?" "Would I rather do something else?" "What would I do if I wasn't afraid?" "What would I do if I had more courage?"

You could ask yourself any powerful, potentially transformative questions. A poem can find and surface these questions, bring them out of the shadows and into the open. They confront you. They demand a hearing and won't be denied.

I like poetry for many reasons: poems say something true, something wise, or something beautiful and memorable. Poetry saves me in some way. I often look for poems to include in a Poetry Table that meet these criteria. I am looking for accessibility. There isn't time at a Poetry Table to solve a poetry puzzle or deal with poems that are too long. The purpose is to interest people in poetry. Another purpose is to give readers an opportunity to find a poem they can relate to, that opens them up to something significant in their lives that they can then share with the people in their small group.

Yet I can relate to non-poets about poetry. Many people have been turned off to it. High school English may have done the turning off, with its frequent focus on outside-in meaning of teacher-selected poems. Society and culture may have turned people away from poetry since it is not seen as utilitarian or practical. Nevertheless, poetry is as essential to a full, well-lived life as are many non-measurable things: music, sunsets, and love. Poems add beauty, spiritual sustenance, and depth to life. They address an invaluable and immeasurable part of the human experience. Poetry fills a void.

Participants don't need to know anything about poetry for a Poetry Table to work. Being human is enough. It helps for the reader to be open and willing to take emotional risks. Ironically, people who study and write poetry can let their knowledge interfere with their Poetry Table experience. I've seen it happen a few times. These individuals may pick poems they already like rather than poems that represent their here and now. They may show off their knowledge and expertise. Their competency or ego may get in their way of being vulnerable or increased self-awareness.

Most of the people reading the poems are not used to poetic devices: rhythm, line breaks, and alliteration. They are not used to the subtleties of poetry, to reading distilled and condensed language. The poems need to be relatable. Part of the idea of a Poetry Table is to give readers a positive, unexpected, unique experience that piques their curiosity about poetry and maybe, just maybe, makes them want to learn more about a poet or buy a poetry book. People let me know these things happen. This is a good thing, a great thing, a terrific additional outcome from a Poetry Table.

FACILITATION

Chapters 13, 14, 15, 16, 17, 18, and 19 address the nuts and bolts of running a Poetry Table. They contain many nuances and considerations I have learned over the years of doing Poetry Tables.

CHAPTER 13

Contracting

SO, LET'S PRETEND ONE morning I get a call from a potential client asking me to discuss a team-building or a leadership program. Right away, I assume I am going to do a Poetry Table at some point in the program. It's a given with me. I may not tell my contact that I will. Most don't care about that level of activity specificity. They are more concerned about outcomes and results. And since I include Poetry Tables in programs with other activities first, I reserve the right to include them if I think the group will benefit and exclude them if the trust level isn't where I want it to be.

On occasion, I've received a request from a trusted facilitator friend who asks me to do a Poetry Table with a group they are working with. I've granted these requests. More often than not, these Poetry Tables have been part of a half-day program that is part of a longer program. The facilitator has already been working with the group and has a high level of trust before I work with them.

With the publication of this book, I may receive calls or emails asking me to do Poetry Tables alone. As I consider the request, I'll still insist on a day-long program, at least, during which a Poetry Table is an option later in the day after I have done other activities and assessed the group's trust level.

CHAPTER 14

What Makes a Good Facilitator?

TO EXCEL AS A Poetry Table facilitator takes time, experience, talent, and self-awareness. I use the term facilitator, but this also applies to other professionals—teachers, therapists, trainers—leading Poetry Tables. While each facilitator has their own style based on individual temperament, personality, interests, skills, and gifts, successful facilitators tend to have certain attributes and skills:

- Instrument of Positive Change
- Able to Get Out of the Way
- Convener, Host, and Holder of Space
- Facilitator of Trust
- Has High-Touch Skills
- Embraces the Spirit of *Educare*
- Shows Humility
- Asks Questions
- Avoids Advice Giving
- Shows Emotional Intelligence and Sensing
- Listens

INSTRUMENT OF POSITIVE CHANGE

I can't expect others to do what I am not willing to do myself. I need to have done a Poetry Table myself before I expect you to do one. I have to be the instrument of change before I expect you to change.

ABLE TO GET OUT OF THE WAY

It's important for the facilitator to get out of the way. A question every facilitator should ask is "Whose needs am I serving, mine or the group's?" An experienced facilitator serves the group's needs.

I don't read or recite poetry before doing Poetry Tables with groups, and I don't say much about poetry before doing one. I give them an opportunity for a powerful experience and, afterwards, ask open-ended questions so they can talk about it and relate it to their life and work. I follow the experiential learning cycle of do, reflect, interpret, and apply.

Most people need space, time, and structure to have their voice heard and to hear other's voices so they can have meaningful conversations. In my team-building or community-building programs, participants might be talking as much as 75% of the time, and in my management and leadership programs it might be 50–75%. Activities, responding to open-ended questions, and small-group participation effectively engages people. It shifts the focus from the facilitator to the participants.

CONVENER, HOST, AND HOLDER OF SPACE

The role of a Poetry Table facilitator is a convener and a holder of psychologically and emotionally safe space. The facilitator gathers people and creates a safe space for them to overcome isolation and learn more about themselves and each other. They offer people powerful experiences within that safe space.

Below are the small-group guidelines I use. They are also principles of practice of a Poetry Table experience. A good Poetry Table facilitator models them. I introduce them at the beginning of any program or workshop, that includes or doesn't include a Poetry Table, and reintroduce them at subsequent sessions. I believe they help create a safe space. I triple emphasize listening in the guidelines because I believe to listen deeply, consistently, and attentively is incredibly difficult.

I have them on a flip-chart page on the wall and in the agenda.

- Listen
- Listen to learn
- Listen to understand
- Be curious
- Ask good questions
- Substitute curiosity and inquiry for advice
- Participate
- Contribute
- Take safe psychological and emotional risks
- Use thoughtful judgment and discretion
- Maintain confidentiality: "What's said in the small group stays in the small group."
- Summarize/confirm and verify: Play back what you have heard. It is the only way we know that understanding is being generated between the parties

Every meeting room has physical and psychological dimensions. The psychological and emotional space in the room can be small or expansive, threatening or safe. As the host, the facilitator creates a welcoming and inviting environment in which the "other" overcomes isolation and has their voice heard. As a facilitator, you want as large a psychological space as possible for all people to fully enter. I'll say more about how to create a psychological safe space in chapter 15.

FACILITATOR OF TRUST

A good facilitator is socially aware, manages relationships, and facilitates trust. With a Poetry Table, you can't eliminate emotional risk. To the contrary, risk is necessary to grow and, in human relationships, ever-present. Eliminating risk or the possibility of betrayal drains the meaning from any experience that evokes vulnerability.

And yet, a good facilitator must use sound judgment and have safeguards so people's feelings aren't hurt. Good judgment takes into account the group's readiness and the right time in the progression of things to do a Poetry Table. The small-group guidelines used during activities and exercises are part of establishing the safeguards to build trust. Still, participants at a Poetry Table need to feel empowered to use their discretion about what and when they want to share. No one is forced to share.

HAS HIGH-TOUCH SKILLS

A good facilitator has high-touch skills. They have a strong awareness of human complexity and are sensitive to the unlimited variability of human beings. They take into account the incredible range of personalities and the subtleties of group dynamics. They bring a personal touch for each and every human.

EMBRACES THE SPIRIT OF EDUCARE

In the spirit of *educare*, the facilitator is the group process expert, not an expert of what direction a participant should take with their life. The facilitator is not the advice giver, a sage in front of the room, or a guru. A good Poetry Table facilitator isn't there to tell frequent anecdotes or clarify a poem's meaning. They keep the focus on the participants and their needs.

SHOWS HUMILITY

A good facilitator is humble and approaches Poetry Tables not knowing what is best for another person. I am reminded of a poem by Jane Hirshfield.

Against Certainty

There is something out in the dark that wants to correct us.
Each time I think "this," it answers "that."
Answers hard, in the heart-grammar's strictness.

If I then say "that," it too is taken away.

Between certainty and the real, an ancient enmity.
When the cat waits in the path-hedge,
no cell of her body is not waiting.
This is how she is able so completely to disappear.

I would like to enter the silence portion as she does.

To live amid the great vanishing as a cat must live,
one shadow fully at ease inside another.

Jane Hirshfield

An attitude of "not knowing" leads to new questions and is at the core of great discoveries and inventions. Being insatiably curious is inspirational.

ASKS QUESTIONS

A great way to maintain focus on participants is to ask open-ended questions. This is one of the most important facilitation skills. Ask a question, be quiet, let people talk, listen to what they say, be curious, and listen for the next question to ask. I'll say more about how to construct good open-ended questions in chapter 18.

AVOIDS ADVICE GIVING

Everyone in the group has innate wisdom. Each person has their own path, journey, and gradient. A problem with giving advice is that the advice may come from the advice-giver's path, what worked for their journey. But the other person is not on that journey. It is more respectful for the facilitator and group members to ask questions than give advice, which most people don't want. What they do want is to be listened to, respected, and heard.

SHOWS EMOTIONAL INTELLIGENCE AND SENSING

One definition of emotional intelligence is . . .

> your ability to recognize and understand emotions in yourself and others, and your ability to use this awareness to manage

your behavior and relationships. Emotional intelligence is the "something" in each of us that is a bit intangible. It affects how we manage behavior, navigate social complexities, and make personal decisions that achieve positive results.

A good Poetry Table facilitator is self-aware and socially aware. They have high emotional intelligence, are adaptable, and can sense what is needed next. A good facilitator monitors and manages their mood and energy and the mood and energy of the group and knows how to assess, adapt, improvise, and adjust accordingly. A training plan or design for a group is a good idea, but you must be flexible enough to shift at a moment's notice if the group needs something else.

LISTENS

One of the most important human and leadership skills is active listening. Poetry Tables, like much of my work, are participant-centered. A good facilitator creates ways for the participants to talk with and listen to each other. This gives the power to the participants rather than the facilitator.

Any facilitator can overtalk, especially people with a preference for extroversion. More extroverted facilitators have to monitor themselves. My motto is "Just say enough." The clock is always ticking. While it is ticking, who is talking? The facilitator or the participants? If the facilitator is talking, then the participants aren't. The experience can be like watching television where the viewer is passive instead of active.

How much to talk is guided by and governed by the context. For instance, in an English classroom or continuing education poetry class, I will talk more than I do during a Poetry Table. In that setting, I am not a facilitator. I am an instructor, and people are there to learn about the poets and their poems. The purpose of the continuing education class isn't primarily *educare*. It may still contain elements of self-discovery, but the purpose of the class is mostly to gain knowledge outside in.

CHAPTER 15

Assessing and Creating a Safe Space

ALTHOUGH I HAVE MENTIONED the importance of creating a safe emotional and psychological space in previous chapters, the topic needs a chapter on its own to emphasize its essential importance. A Poetry Table can be a throwaway experience like anything else if it is facilitated poorly. Worse, the experience can be harmful and damaging if the table—the space—isn't set properly.

READINESS

The Poetry Table is not an introductory or beginning activity for groups. It is not low risk. There is emotional exposure. Powerful feelings may come up, including tears. I don't do it before I detect a level of trust in a work group. I wait to do it later, after doing other trust and relationship-building activities, such as personality styles assessments or personal history exercises.

There is always a range of readiness within any group. I have to make a judgment call if enough people are ready and if the room feels psychologically safe. Poetry Tables work best if people are open to self-disclosing. It works well to either develop or already have decent trust and psychological safety in the room. A Poetry Table is a good fit if there are positive, supportive, and healthy or, at least, neutral relationships between people. All facilitators have to make judgment calls if people are ready for any risky activity, especially Poetry Tables.

I have done Poetry Tables on the first night of my continuing education classes. The people in the classes are strangers to each other so they don't have a negative history or emotional baggage with each other like some people could if they worked together or if they were in a therapy group. Additionally, the primary purpose of a Poetry Table with a class is to introduce the poets to the class. Building class connections is an added benefit.

The same thing is true in an elementary school classroom. The primary purpose of a Poetry Table in a school setting, most of the time, would be to introduce poetry in a fresh way.

Nevertheless, we don't know what is going on inside a person, any person. Every person brings a personal history to a Poetry Table. A poem can touch a deep place in a person and could trigger a powerful emotional response. The facilitator needs to be aware of this and be alert and attentive.

INTERVENTION

A facilitator needs to have the courage and willingness to intervene if group members are giving advice, dominating the conversation, or breaking the small-group guidelines in any way. The guidelines need to be discussed and reinforced at each session before a Poetry Table. They become a norm for the group's interactions. It's imperative to establish these as understood and accepted group norms in the training or team building before doing a Poetry Table.

During an actual Poetry Table, it can be difficult for a facilitator to intervene because at this stage of group interaction, I usually have each small group leave the large group room and go to a private space to read and converse. The small groups manage themselves and self-facilitate. The private space allows for more intimacy. I haven't seen a problem occur with the small groups as long as the small-group guidelines have been established and the directions and questions in the Invitation Sheet are clear. People of all ages tend to be supportive and respectful of their peers.

CHAPTER 16

Choosing Poems

IT IS IMPORTANT TO have a wide variety of poems for a Poetry Table, as well as a range of voices and themes. The poems chosen should be relevant to why the group is convening to do a Poetry Table. For lists of poems for different groups, please see the Appendix. Two excellent resources for finding poems are poets.org and poetryfoundation.org. Once you have chosen your poems, print them on white paper in twelve-point Times New Roman font. You want them to be easy to read. I don't alter the line breaks or stanzas. I present a poem exactly as the poet published it.

VARIETY AND CHOICE

Eighty to ninety poems for each small group of three to five people is ideal. Each small group has the same poems in the same order in the stack. The order does matter since people naturally tend to read poems at the top of the stack first. The facilitator can tell groups they don't have to read from the top. They can start with poems at the bottom, in the middle, or however they choose.

In my experience, twenty poems don't provide enough variety. You need to have a wide enough range of poems so that at least one interests each reader. It is better to have too many poems in the stack than not enough. I typically include poems by both Nobel Prize in Literature winners and lesser-known poets, and even include a few of my own. A diverse selection is essential. I tell groups, "The goal isn't for you to read all of the poems or even most of them. The goal is to read at your own pace in the time given and to find at least one poem you can relate to." With more poems, the odds increase that each reader will find one they like.

How I conduct Poetry Tables has evolved. In the early days, as I was experimenting with different ways of bringing poems into work groups, I sometimes chose a single poem for people to reflect upon and talk about. I quickly realized that approach didn't work for many people. No matter how great the poem, how much I liked it, or how much it fit the context, it didn't appeal to everyone. It didn't ring true to their here and now.

I recall an experience facilitating a planning meeting in January 2010 for a fatherhood forum. I picked the following William Stafford poem.

With Kit, Age 7, At the Beach

We would climb the highest dune,
from there to gaze and come down:
the ocean was performing;
we contributed our climb.

Waves leapfrogged and came
straight out of the storm.
What should our gaze mean?
Kit waited for me to decide.

Standing on such a hill,
what would you tell your child?
That was an absolute vista.
Those waves raced far, and cold.

'How far could you swim, Daddy,
in such a storm?'
'As far as was needed,' I said,
and as I talked, I swam.

William Stafford

Since the poem is about a positive vision of fatherhood, and the reason for the gathering was to discuss and enhance positive visions of fatherhood, I thought it was an ideal one to share. Many people liked the poem. Some didn't. My experience has been that whenever I pick a poem for other people, there will be some who won't like the poem no matter what I say about it. When people have choices—when they pick a poem that matters to them—they will more likely discover its relevance.

When a poem is picked for everyone, group-think and herd acceptance are hazards. People may say they like the poem; they may want to find something to like about it even though they wouldn't have picked it if given a choice. There's even a tendency for some people to be agreeable and say they like something because it is the only choice they are given.

When a poem is picked for people, they may adjust their truth to accommodate the group and facilitator. With choice, I am confident each person will find the poem they need. Almost any poem a person chooses will work because, it bears repeating, humans contain multitudes.

LENGTH OF THE POEMS

For all their merits, some poems are too long and can't be understood quickly. I might use them with school groups or continuing education classes where we have more time and classes to examine and discuss longer poems, but for most Poetry Tables, my rule of thumb is to offer poems that are fairly short. Some are one stanza. Most are less than one page. A few are two pages or a bit longer.

Sometimes I include an excerpt from a long poem. I like T. S. Elliot's "Four Quartets," but it is far too long for most Poetry Tables and, even if the poem was short, it is not easily accessible to people unfamiliar with poetry. I often, though, use excerpts from it, like this one.

From Little Gidding

We shall not cease from exploration
And the end of all our exploring
Will be to arrive where we started
And know the place for the first time.

T. S. Elliot

WHITE SPACE

A poem's look matters. All poems, especially the longer ones I include, tend to have a lot of white space. White spaces allow the reader to slow down, breathe, and reflect. They allow the words to resonate within the reader.

Poems with white space, short lines, and short stanzas can be inviting. A big block of words isn't as inviting. A long stanza, followed by more long ones, even if they are full of images and ideas, can be intimidating. A couple of poems I have cited here—Anne Sexton's

"Courage" and Wislawa Szymborska's "A Few Words on the Soul"—are examples of longer poems with short lines, many stanzas, and plenty of white space.

A commonly chosen poem among architects, land use planners, historic preservationists, and other professionals concerned with private and public spaces is Lao Tzu's "The Uses of Not."

The Uses of Not

Thirty spokes
meet in the hub.
Where the wheel isn't
is where it's useful.

Hollowed out,
clay makes a pot.
Where the pot's not
is where it's useful.

Cut doors and windows
to make a room.
Where the room isn't,
there's room for you.

So the profit in what is
is in the use of what isn't.

Lao Tzu

ACCESSIBILITY

Most poems that I choose are accessible, which doesn't mean they're dumbed down. Accessible poems can be intelligent and address complex issues. From my perspective, "accessible" means the poems address common human concerns with language that echoes everyday speech. The language isn't necessarily verbatim to common speech. It is constructed. There is a form and an art to it. It is a poem, after all. The words are intentionally arranged.

Accessible poems aren't written primarily for other poets or to address the poetic tribe's insular concerns. They are bigger in scope, more universal.

Accessible also means the poems address truths about life. Sometimes those truths are hard. Here is a terrific, bitingly honest poem about human truths.

A Contribution to Statistics

Out of a hundred people

those who always know better
– fifty-two,

doubting every step
– nearly all the rest,

glad to lend a hand
if it doesn't take too long
– as high as forty-nine,

always good
because they can't be otherwise
– four, well maybe five,

able to admire without envy
– eighteen,

suffering illusions
induced by fleeting youth
– sixty, give or take a few,

not to be taken lightly
– forty and four,

living in constant fear
of someone or something
– seventy-seven,

capable of happiness
– twenty-something tops,

harmless singly,
savage in crowds
– half at least,

cruel
when forced by circumstances
– better not to know
even ballpark figures,

wise after the fact
– just a couple more
than wise before it,

taking only things from life
– thirty
(I wish I were wrong),

hunched in pain,
no flashlight in the dark
– eighty-three
sooner or later,

righteous
– thirty-five, which is a lot,

righteous
and understanding
– three,

worthy of compassion
– ninety-nine,

mortal

– a hundred out of a hundred.
Thus far this figure still remains unchanged.

Wislawa Szymborska

TITLES

People in the non-profit world commonly pick "A Contribution to Statistics." Most say they are drawn to the poem by the title, the word "statistics," and then the journey of the poem surprises them. It takes a turn, and another and another, and keeps taking turns, exploring, extending, and deepening its witty and bitingly honest examination of human nature.

"A Contribution to Statistics" is also an excellent example of a poem with a lot of white space, short lines, and many stanzas. It is easy to enter the poem's language-world. At the same time, it is a complex world without easy answers that Szymborska is inviting the reader to contemplate.

Here is a Marge Piercy poem with straightforward language and a theme that appeals to many people doing practical work.

To Be of Use

The people I love the best
jump into work head first
without dallying in the shallows
and swim off with sure strokes almost out of sight.
They seem to become natives of that element,
the black sleek heads of seals
bouncing like half-submerged balls.

I love people who harness themselves, an ox to a heavy cart,
who pull like water buffalo, with massive patience,
who strain in the mud and the muck to move things forward,
who do what has to be done, again and again.

I want to be with people who submerge
in the task, who go into the fields to harvest
and work in a row and pass the bags along,
who are not parlor generals and field deserters
but move in the common rhythm
when the food must come in or the fire be put out.

The work of the world is common as mud.
Botched, it smears the hands, crumbles to dust.
But the thing worth doing well done
has a shape that satisfies, clean and evident.
Greek amphoras for wine or oil,
Hopi vases that held corn, are put in museums
but you know they were made to be used.
The pitcher cries for water to carry
and a person for work that is real.

    Marge Piercy

I remember facilitating a Poetry Table with water treatment operators from a water diversion plant. There were sixteen people in the group with four people at each table. Each table had the same stack of poems. Each stack contained one copy of "To Be of Use." It was picked by one operator at each table.

What initially drew the operators to the poem was the title. An interesting, relevant, or intriguing title can be the doorway to a person's interest in reading a poem. In an accessible poem, the language that follows keeps inviting the reader in.

A RANGE OF VOICES AND THEMES

Most Poetry Table groups I have worked with have been work groups, although I've also conducted them with church groups, school groups, and students in continuing education poetry classes. It is important to tailor the selection of poems to a group, to make them relevant. Nevertheless, selecting poems for a group is always something of a guessing game. I have poems that are reliably picked and predictably touch many lives. "Kindness," "Courage," Don't Quit," and "The Way It Is" are examples. They have universal appeal.

Each group may have themes that interest them, some of which seem obvious. I am not going to include animal poems for a group of working adults. However, I will include them with seven-year-old kids, many of whom have pets or stuffed animals and are intrigued by them.

It is essential to consider the context when picking poems. A short list of questions I might ask my group contact are about purpose and outcomes:

- Why is the group gathering?
- What is the purpose of the gathering?
- What desired outcomes do you want?

If I was doing a Poetry Table with a group of military veterans who were gathered as a group for the purpose of working together to solve a veterans-related issue, I would certainly include some poems that have to do with the experience of serving, of military sacrifice, and of being in combat. It doesn't mean every, or any, veteran would pick a poem that has to do with serving, combat, or war, but it is a possibility.

Their service may not be the dominant theme in their lives. They may be more present in the here and now, the moment during which they are reading. Poems that address different themes might be more relevant. I can't assume to know what people will pick and so make educated guesses. Sometimes I am right. More often than not, I am surprised.

Every stack of poems needs to include a range of themes, addressing the immense range of human experiences. Poetry Tables are a way for me to introduce readers to some of my favorite poets and some of my favorite poems. I include other poems because I think they will fit and find a home with some readers.

I include a mix of poetic voices. It is crucial to have poems by people from many different backgrounds and cultures, many different experiences and voices. One wants the participants to see themselves and each other in the poets. Since I live in New Mexico, if I had a group that was all or part Native American, then I would certainly have some poems from Native American poets, with Native American voices and perspectives on how to live life. As with military veterans or seven-year-old children, it doesn't mean that a Native American will pick a poem by a Native American poet or that a woman will pick a poem by a woman poet and so on. Humans aren't so predictable.

Regardless of the group, a Poetry Table is a good opportunity to stretch people's ideas of poetry, offer fresh or unheard perspectives and voices, and introduce poems from diverse backgrounds and cultures. Here is a lovely poem by Joy Harjo, the first Native American United States Poet Laureate.

Eagle Poem

To pray you open your whole self
To sky, to earth, to sun, to moon
To one whole voice that is you.
And know there is more

That you can't see, can't hear;
Can't know except in moments
Steadily growing, and in languages
That aren't always sound but other
Circles of motion.
Like eagle that Sunday morning
Over Salt River. Circled in blue sky
In wind, swept our hearts clean
With sacred wings.
We see you, see ourselves and know
That we must take the utmost care
And kindness in all things.
Breathe in, knowing we are made of
All this, and breathe, knowing
We are truly blessed because we
Were born, and die soon within a
True circle of motion,
Like eagle rounding out the morning
Inside us.
We pray that it will be done
In beauty.
In beauty.

Joy Harjo

I am confident people will select what they need, what reflects their inner life, and will transcend the narrow confines of identity categories. Sometimes a Hispanic person will pick a poem by a Hispanic poet, but not always, not even close to always, and maybe they pick the poem not because the poem is by a Hispanic poet, per se, but because they can relate to a theme in the poem. At the end of the day, I want people to find at least one poem they can relate to.

UNIVERSALITY

Most of the poems I select are about the challenges and joys of being human. I aim for universal themes and common human experiences: not quitting, persevering, death, becoming older, getting old, being a parent, courage, grief, kindness, loneliness, finding one's way and path in life.

The language can be colloquial, as in this example by Langston Hughes.

Mother to Son

Well, son, I'll tell you:
Life for me ain't been no crystal stair.
It's had tacks in it,
And splinters,
And boards torn up,
And places with no carpet on the floor—
Bare.
But all the time
I'se been a-climbin' on,
And reachin' landin's,
And turnin' corners,
And sometimes goin' in the dark
Where there ain't been no light.
So boy, don't you turn back.
Don't you set down on the steps
'Cause you finds it's kinder hard.
Don't you fall now—
For I'se still goin,' honey,
I'se still climbin,'
And life for me ain't been no crystal stair.

Langston Hughes

This is an excellent poem about sacrifice, overcoming hardship, and being persistent. It touches upon many themes for a huge range of readers. Langston Hughes grew up in the Midwest and lived most of his adult life in Harlem. One doesn't have to be African American or from Harlem to like it. Great poetry crosses boundaries. Many people from a range of races and social and economic backgrounds relate to "Mother to Son." Its language is direct, straightforward, and powerful because it speaks to the humanity in us all. The communication of love in it is beautiful, awesome.

CHAPTER 17

How to Run a Poetry Table – A Step-by-Step Summary

1. Place a stack of eighty to ninety poems in the middle of each table.

2. Ask everyone to grab a handful of poems and read them in silence. Say: "If a poem appeals to you and you like it, then place it aside in a personal stack. If a poem doesn't, then put it back in the middle of the table for others to read."

3. Let people read in silence for ten to twelve minutes.

4. Monitor that people are reading and putting poems aside.

5. After ten to twelve minutes, tell them to pick the poem from their personal stack that they like the most, that matters to them the most.

6. Hand out the Invitation Sheet.

7. Read the Invitation Sheet to them.

8. Model reading poems slowly.

9. Let them read their poems in their small groups and answer the questions on the Invitation Sheet.

10. Walk around to see how they are doing and how the timing is going.

11. As they are finishing up, remind them of the Appreciations section on the Invitation Sheet.

12. Reconvene as a large group.

13. Ask them: "What was valuable for you about that experience?"

14. Have a conversation.

15. Afterwards, invite up to three people to take a turn and read their poems and share their answers to the Invitation Sheet questions.

16. Later in the program day or in subsequent program days, invite other people to read their poems and share their answers.

CHAPTER 18

Poetry Tables – Considerations, Nuances, and Details

To see a world in a Grain of Sand
And a Heaven in a Wild Flower
Hold Infinity in the palm of your hand
And Eternity in an hour.

From "Auguries of Innocence" by William Blake

LITTLE THINGS IN POETRY Tables matter. Attention to detail matters. The little things are not incidental. The details of the room arrangements, the setting, the small-group guidelines, the degree of emotional safety, and how questions are constructed are significant because they individually, collectively, and cumulatively impact Poetry Table experiences.

SELF-DISCLOSURE

"What will and must be spoken."

Ralph Waldo Emerson

Emerson also said, "It is a secret that can no longer be kept secret, a way of knowing." Emerson was talking to the maker of a poem about the writing of a poem. It also relates to the reading of a poem. Part of a Poetry Table experience is to share something that is not known to others in the small group. The hidden doesn't have to be because of shame or distrust. I don't assign a negative motive for why someone hasn't shared. It could be as simple as the right occasion hasn't occurred. Perhaps there hasn't been an opening. A Poetry Table can be the door into the depths and the catalyst for conversation. Each person still retains the choice whether to self-disclose. A Poetry Table is a place, ideally a safe space, to reveal what is hidden and acknowledge out loud something true about the self.

SILENCE AND SPEECH

Both silence and speech are integral elements of a Poetry Table experience. Everyone reads the poems in silence, which for most people is a rare event in life. To read soulful words in the presence of other humans can be a powerful, profound experience. Reading the poems in the silence of others allows for a reflective moment and disciplined stillness. The moment often feels like a gift.

The silence while reading can allow memories to surface and can be a doorway to a deep well of wisdom. Perhaps you are at a crossroads, a junction. Do you go this way with your life or that way? Perhaps you have been avoiding a big question or an essential conversation. "Would

I be better off if I looked for another job, if I addressed this scary thing with my wife, mother, father, sister?" "What if I apologized to this person or that person?" "What if I took the risk and started my own business?" "What if I fulfilled a dream and wrote the book I have been putting off?" The list of questions and possibilities is endless.

I am reminded of the wonderful Pablo Neruda poem "Keeping quiet." I often include it in a Poetry Table.

Keeping Quiet

Now we will count to twelve
and we will all keep still.

For once on the face of the earth,
let's not speak any language;
let's stop for one second,
and not move our arms so much.

It would be an exotic moment,
without rush, without engines;
we would all be together
in a sudden strangeness.

Fishermen in the cold sea
would not harm whales
and the man gathering salt
would look at his hurt hands.

Those who prepare green wars,
wars with gas, wars with fire,
victories with no survivors,
would put on clean clothes
and walk about with their brothers
in the shade, doing nothing.

What I want should not be confused
with total inactivity.

Life is what it is about:
I want no truck with death.

If we were not so single-minded
about keeping our lives moving,
and for once could do nothing,
perhaps a huge silence
might interrupt this sadness
of never understanding ourselves
and of threatening ourselves with death.
Perhaps the earth can teach us
as when everything seems dead
and later proves to be alive.

Now I'll count up to twelve
and you keep quiet and I will go.

Pablo Neruda

Poetry Tables value depth over speed. It is a chance to slow down, stop racing from one thing to another, or switching from one electronic device to another. It is an opportunity to rest the pinball brain and reflect.

For some people this stillness is liberating. Those addicted to frequent stimulation may be uncomfortable. For some, especially too often young adults, being alone with their thoughts and feelings for a long period of time is unfamiliar or scary, so they distract themselves from themselves by checking their phones. Poetry Tables are counter-cultural. They push against prevailing norms.

MODEL THE WAY

Reading the poems in silence can be calming. The room becomes quiet and more peaceful. After people read and have selected a poem, they are invited to read the poem twice out loud to their small-group members. That's the invitation. They read it however they want. My only request is to ask them to read it twice and slowly. I don't ask them to read it dramatically or with any special attention to line breaks. This isn't a professional poetry reading class or an acting class. I want to stay away from "right" ways of reading.

I model reading a poem slowly out loud. I'll pick a short poem from a stack and read it slowly twice. I'll read it slowly, then slower on the second reading. I want to emphasize the importance of reading the poem twice and slowly. Modeling these behaviors increases the odds that everyone will do them in their small groups. Without modeling them, some people will only read their poem once in the small group and rush through reading it.

Reading the poem is a chance to hear it out loud and feel it deeply. I want them to hear their own voice, to hear and embody the energy and emotion. I want others to experience the same. By reading the poem twice, readers tend to reveal what touches them. The second reading helps break through defenses.

MEANING FROM WITHIN

Sharing why your poem matters to you is what is important, rather than analyzing it. Analysis undermines the experience. The poem, as it is written, and why it moves its reader, is more interesting than the analysis. The person lending personal meaning to the poem is also interesting.

A Poetry Table deals with many invisible elements. As a facilitator, I can only see what I see, hear what I hear. If there is emotion at a table, if people talk longer and more openly, then I might assume they are having a more powerful experience than people who aren't expressing emotion or talking as much. This interpretation, however, may not be true. Someone may not show their emotion, but they may be deeply moved. Many people have expressed later in writing how deeply they were affected by the experience.

"Red Brocade," the poem in the Introduction, is inviting. I use the term *invitation* with Poetry Tables. I like its hospitable and welcoming tone. "You are invited to do this." The Invitation Sheet invites them to read their poem twice to their small group and to answer the questions. Participants are invited to share appreciations at the end. Invitation also honors psychological safety and evokes community. A Poetry Table can build a sense of community in line with other aspects of the program and the reasons the group is participating in a Poetry Table in the first place.

A PHYSICAL ACT

"If I read a book and it makes my whole body so cold no fire can ever warm me, I know that is poetry. If I feel physically as if the top of my head were taken off, I know that is poetry. These are the only ways I know it."

Emily Dickinson

Emily Dickinson is struck by the physicality of reading poetry. Reading poetry and then reading a poem out loud and talking about it are physical acts. They are somatic acts, embodied experiences. A poem can stun, surprise, strike like a thunderbolt. For any reader, the right poem can be a wake-up call.

In Poetry Tables, people are asked to read their poem twice out loud in their small group. Hearing the poems read slowly is an embodied experience for both reader and listeners. It can have a mantra-like quality and enhances concentration and focus. We feel it deep inside.

THE POEM AS A FOIL – THE CRUX OF THE MATTER

The poem can be a form of deflection, a type of foil, and an essential companion. It's a separate thing that takes the attention off you. This is the crux of the matter, the alchemy of the experience. The initial focus is on the words and form, the sound of it. People may be willing to self-disclose because they are talking about the poem, not themselves. But, eventually, they are talking about themselves, often directly. Without the poem as a companion, they might not speak so openly. They might not talk about themselves in the same way without the poem. More reticent and more introverted people may not speak at all. The engineer who read "Kindness" to the large group probably wouldn't have spoken without the poem as his companion.

THE PLEASURE OF LANGUAGE

> What is pronounced strengthens itself.
> What is not pronounced tends to nonexistence.

> Czeslaw Milosz, from "Reading the Japanese Poet Issa"

The sound of words is an early pleasure in being human. Babies and toddlers love the sound of their own voices, the sound of language, the sounds of their parents and pets. They like rhyming. Sounds are enchanting. Powerful language works its way inside a person. People will often say about a speech that they don't remember what the speaker said, but they remember how she made them feel. Poetic sounds and words find a home inside us. They stick. "The Wolf at Two A.M." stuck inside the manager for many years. "Accounting" stuck inside my cousin for twenty-one years.

A person speaking out loud is making a form of declaration. The speaker is standing for something. The act of speaking can be courageous and transformative. In essence, the speaker may be saying, "There, I finally said it, not only to myself, but to the world."

THE RIGHT TO SAY NO

It is okay for people at a Poetry Table to say no. Too often people feel coerced in organizations, believing they can't say no. Although I prefer for everyone to speak and share their poem, the invitation in the Invitation Sheet is exactly that—an invitation. For it to be genuine, a person must have a choice, the option to say no and not read their poem.

Yet almost everyone reads their poems. Over the years, I recall no more than ten or fewer people who did not read in the small group, often because they told their small group they would be overcome with emotion if they read the poem aloud. I remember a librarian from a New Mexico state agency feeling overwhelmed by the poem because it reminded her of the death of her husband. She asked another person in the small group to read her poem and let the group know why she didn't want to read. Initially, she didn't answer the Invitation Sheet's questions. Later, after more people in her group read and talked about their poems, she collected herself and said more about the poem and her relationship to it.

Someone has to read and talk first in the small group. I never establish an order with reading and talking. Someone volunteers. This could be seen as an act of leadership or courage. The experience can be generative and reciprocal as one person in the small group speaks openly, honestly, and courageously, which may allow—give permission to—others to speak authentically and courageously.

I am reminded of a poem by Vaclav Havel, the playwright, who also was the President of the Czech Republic.

It Is I Who Must Begin

It is I who must begin.
Once I begin, once I try—
here and now,
right where I am,
not excusing myself
by saying that things
would be easier elsewhere,
without grand speeches and
ostentatious gestures,
but all the more persistently
– to live in harmony
with the "voice of Being," as I
understand it within myself
– as soon as I begin that,
I suddenly discover,
to my surprise, that
I am neither the only one,
nor the first,
nor the most important one
to have set out
upon that road.

Whether all is really lost
or not depends entirely on
whether or not I am lost.

Vaclav Havel

A person who is hesitant or nervous about sharing may go after someone else starts and sets the tone. I trust that people will say what they need to say and go as deep as they need to go. As the activity begins, I encourage people to take risks, contribute, and be courageous. I don't say something like "the person who is feeling the most emotional should go first." That is too manipulative.

PAYING ATTENTION

"Attention is the rarest and purest form of generosity."
Simone Weil

Below is a poem that addresses people's need to be listened to and their yearning to be heard.

When Someone Deeply Listens to You

When someone deeply listens to you
it is like holding out a dented cup
you've had since childhood
and watching it fill up with
cold, fresh water.
When it balances on top of the brim,
you are understood.
When it overflows and touches your skin,
you are loved.

When someone deeply listens to you
the room where you stay
starts a new life
and the place where you wrote
your first poem
begins to glow in your mind's eye.

It is as if gold has been discovered!

When someone deeply listens to you
your bare feet are on the earth
and a beloved land that seemed distant
is now at home within you.

John Fox

We often get in our own way of good listening. We're conditioned to the "next thing" and sometimes miss "the now." We focus on the past or the future. Hearing the poems read out loud slowly allows us to be more present. We know the poem means something special to the reader and listen more attentively than we otherwise might.

Listening well is one of those skills that is never finished, fulfilled, accomplished. There is no mountaintop where one has reached a pinnacle of perfect listening. In Poetry Tables, people are encouraged to be curious about their group members, ask questions, summarize what they believe they heard, and learn more. They are not listening to give advice, to fix things or the other person, nor to solve anything for their group members, or rescue or save them.

LIBERATION AND LAUGHTER

Although a perception could be that a Poetry Table is somber, my experience has been that there is much laughter after people share and open up. Sometimes the heartfelt, robust laughter is a release from tension or a reflection of people being free to be themselves.

Many people have said that talking about their poem has a liberating effect. They often have used that word—liberating. They feel freed. They are free to express their inner life, be genuine, and reveal what's in their hearts.

OVERCOMING DEFENSE MECHANISMS

Real relationships are built on connecting to another's humanness and the ability to discuss and share emotions, which are at the heart of most things. A Poetry Table can help people, teams, and groups practice relationship-building skills.

It's easy to have superficial conversations. It happens all the time. It doesn't take much effort to talk about sports, the weather, and celebrities. Conversations that evoke real emotion can be more challenging.

Not discussing or showing feelings may be a defense mechanism. It can be a way to stay guarded, defended, and protected. Being dismissive of another person's vulnerability can be a way of hiding insecurities. With a Poetry Table, I am striving for people to be authentic and to overcome reflexive and programmed defenses to safety and trust. If people cannot be vulnerable, they cannot get far in relationships. Real relationships are rarely built on competency, even at work. They are built on trust and mutuality.

SAYING LESS MAY BE MORE – MINIMIZING EXPECTATIONS

Most of the time when I work with groups, participants don't know they are going to take part in a Poetry Table until just before they are doing it. I don't advertise or broadcast that the next time we are together we are going to read poetry and then talk about it. This might create panic. I think saying less is more, at first, with poetry. I don't say anything. I just do a Poetry Table.

When I directed challenge course programs, we had an informed consent talk first. The participants needed to be told about the physical part, the need to wear clothes suitable to the activities and the weather, and the real and perceived physical risks. You don't need to have an informed consent talk before doing a Poetry Table.

A Poetry Table is physically accessible. It is inclusive. People can be wearing any kind of clothes and be any size. None of the external conditions matters. It's all internal: emotions, mind, and spirit.

DIRECTNESS AND INDIRECTNESS

A Poetry Table is a way of doing what Emily Dickinson suggests in her poem "Tell all the truth but tell it slant." Her poem speaks, in part, to poetry's indirectness.

Tell all the truth but tell it slant—(1263)

Tell all the truth but tell it slant—
Success in Circuit lies
Too bright for our infirm Delight
The Truth's superb surprise
As Lightning to the Children eased
With explanation kind
The Truth must dazzle gradually
Or every man be blind—

Emily Dickinson

There are places in life for directness and closed yes-or-no questions. Did you send the email? Did you brush your teeth? Did you take the dog for a walk? Sometimes this direct approach works. Other times, it creates defensiveness. A Poetry Table may be a way around those defenses—a sideways, indirect approach to allowing people let down their barriers and be authentic. By talking about their poem, they talk about themselves. The exercise is as much about the person as it is about the poem—actually, more so, because no two people will talk about the same poem in the same way. They share what the poem means to them and how the poem relates to their unique life. They are making it personal.

It is common for someone to say they didn't like a poem, but when someone else reads it and talks about it, they like it. I then often hear: "Can I take a picture of the poem?"

Good poetry isn't reporting. It isn't focused on facts. Indirection—telling things slant and sideways—are central to poetry and to a Poetry Table. The poems and Poetry Table catch people off guard, in a good way. Their defenses aren't engaged because they don't feel at risk. It's not meant to be a gotcha moment or an attempt to trick or deceive. The intent is not malicious. It is, however, an attempt to bypass defenses. People still have the choice to share what they want to share. No one is out to get anyone else, except to "get" people to become authentic. They choose what to disclose. The small-group guidelines encourage people not to fix things for their peers and to substitute curiosity and inquiry for advice.

TIMING

I always hold Poetry Tables at the end of a retreat day or later in a program after the guidelines have been established and people understand "the rules of engagement." I do it after I have had a chance to establish trust and safety in the group, to observe if there are individuals who are undermining trust or giving advice. Over the years I can think of a few people who needed to be talked to privately or who were problematic. They either left a multi-day program, deciding it wasn't for them, or corrected their behavior after I addressed it with them.

People aren't always ready for Poetry Table experiences. I recognize that not everyone is ready or able to be reflective. Some people avoid looking inward. I remember a leadership program with a manager who was aggressively defensive. Everything about him was about being in control, competent, and direct. He wouldn't participate in anything that made him feel vulnerable or dependent. I saw fear, really terror, on his face when we were preparing to do a blindfolded communication activity. He was shaking. I gave him an out and let him be an observer.

He is the exception. Most people participate. "It's not as bad as I feared. In fact, it wasn't bad at all." "It was actually fun and interesting." "I'm glad I did it." I used to hear these comments all the time on the ropes course at Santa Fe Community College. People would make up a story in their head about what the ropes course program was going to be like, what high events they couldn't do. The actual experience was different, which was a lesson in itself for many people about not assuming the worst and making stuff up in life about people, events, and situations.

DEALING WITH PRISONERS

Sometimes I have prisoners, people who don't want to be there, who may initially be resistant or angry. I often address the resistance—the mandatory nature—up front with humor, by saying: "People often come to trainings with one of three attitudes: as prisoners, vacationers, or learners. Whatever your attitude is, you can choose to change it and be a learner. I can't force you to learn. I will give you exercises and experiences that can be valuable and useful if you contribute, participate, and take risks."

If they feel supported, they will open up and participate, and the prisoners may benefit enormously from their experiences. Over the years, I've received so many comments along the lines of "I didn't want to come. I thought it would be stupid, but I'm glad I came. I learned a lot." These comments are more rewarding than hearing from the choir, the people excited to attend. I think for many teachers, educators, trainers, and facilitators, that is often the case. It is rewarding to acknowledge and manage resistance in this way and see a reluctant participant become a learner.

INDIVIDUAL VOICES

One of the fascinating things for me as the facilitator-host is to hear how different people read the same poem in a small group on the same day and have different experiences. If I have sixteen people in the large group, I probably would have four small groups of four, as I did with the water treatment operators I mentioned earlier. Although the words of "To Be of Use" were the same from small group to small group, the four operators who picked it talked about it differently, each relating it to his unique story and life.

With all groups, I move around and listen in a bit on small-group conversations and have heard how differently people encounter a poem. Each person brings their own experiences to the poem. This is also why a person could pass over a poem and then, when a fellow small-group member picks it and talks about it, it is brought to life and connects to other people. The reader completes the poem, bringing to the conversation their own experiences and making the poem interesting to other small-group members, who may not have initially connected with it.

SITTING AT TABLES

Ideally, people sit at round tables where they can see each other. Rectangular tables can also work, though round tables are better because the circle is a holistic space. There is no head of the table. The tables need to be just large enough to have space to put the stack of poems and for each person to create their own personal stack. Large tables like long, oval boardroom tables reduce intimacy because they separate people too much.

SMALL GROUPS

The ideal small group size is four or five people. I have all small groups approximately the same size so they finish around the same time, though it almost never works out exactly that way. If I have twenty people and split them into five groups of four, then the timing might be close. If I have nineteen, then the numbers don't divide exactly and the timing may be off. In any case, even with five groups of four, people talk and process at different speeds, and some people have more to say. Perhaps a poem really hits a deep place and the person has a lot to express.

It's a delicate balance. I'd like each reader to have their say and, ideally, for all groups to finish, more or less, at the same time. I won't cut anyone off. I'd rather see one group finish ahead of another. As I circulate between the groups, I check to see how they are doing and who has taken a turn and who hasn't. If a group finishes ahead of others, I'll let them know and encourage them to chat or talk about other poems in their stack.

Usually, I don't give people a set time to read and talk, for example, "You have three minutes a person." I usually leave it open. My experience has been that it takes five to eight minutes for a person to read his poem twice and answer the four or five questions I've posed. Invariably, after everyone has taken a turn, groups converse more.

Leaving things open-ended can create timing challenges. As the facilitator, if I present content, then I control the time. If I ask open-ended questions, I relinquish control and time to the participants. They are in control. I have shifted the focus and power in the room from me to them.

Personality can play into how long people talk in groups. In larger groups, more extroverted people might be inclined to talk where more introverted people wouldn't. More talkative or expressive groups might want more time. They might like self-disclosing. They might enjoy sharing. Other groups that are more taciturn or reticent might want less time. They may not be used to sharing.

Some groups may be used to yes-or-no questions and live in a community or work in a culture that is prone to less conversational talk or might be temperamentally inclined not to talk much. For instance, I have been in smaller towns and rural communities where people tended to talk less during a Poetry Table. They may not be used to asking each other questions or elaborating on the questions in the Invitation Sheet. Some groups may only answer the questions and not elaborate or expand, even with open-ended questions.

Just because one group talks at length doesn't mean that their individual and group experiences are better than a group that barely answers the questions. It is impossible to know what is beneficial from one person to another. I've had shy or reticent individuals not say much, take their turn, and end the conversation quickly. Later, I would receive an email or a comment in the evaluation sharing how valuable the experience was for them. I understand that people process things in different ways. Some people are more external in their processing. Some are more internal. Being incommunicative or undemonstrative is not an indicator of lack of engagement.

It is better to have too much time than not enough, so it is smart to have a buffer. I would probably allow at least forty minutes for a group of four people. However, some groups may take much longer. Then

I may have to either shorten something else or cut something from the agenda. Facilitators have to use their judgment and skill with being high touch to determine the right thing to do.

GROUP SELECTION

I let people self-select small groups. However, as I have said before, the context matters. If it is a team-building program, then I might say, "Get together with people you need to work with more closely in the future." If it is a community-building or leadership program, then I might say, "Get together with people you haven't been with much or at all. This is a chance to get to know people you don't know well."

Many arrangements work. Even with people who know each other well or have worked together a long time, there can be terrific discoveries. A Poetry Table is a new experience and a chance to have a new conversation between people. We all have hidden areas of our lives that are untapped and can be meaningful to share.

READING TIMES

After the small groups are set up, I allow about ten minutes for them to read the poems. Sometimes a group needs a minute or two longer, which is fine as long as other groups are still engaged and we have time.

Is ten to twelve minutes enough? It can take thirty minutes or more to adjust to the subtle modulations of poetry, but I don't have thirty minutes for most groups. Since the poems I use tend to be short, it is enough. I choose to exclude those poets whose voices are alien to regular speech and to the non-reader's ear and thus require much more time to adjust to, such as Gerard Manley Hopkins and Wallace Stevens.

POWERFUL QUESTIONS

The questions in a Poetry Table may be as important as the poems. Questions spur conversation. The most powerful questions tend not to be yes/no or fact-based. They often begin with "What," "When," "Where," "Why," and "How." They're simple, clear, often penetrating, and they challenge the reader to reflect at a deeper level. Energizing and relevant, they touch upon the reader's values, hope, and ideals.

For example, the following questions have little power:

- Did you like the poem?
- What is the title of the poem?

More powerful open-ended questions:

- What initially drew you to the poem?
- What about the poem matters to you?

After the participants finish reading, I hand out the Invitation Sheet and review it with them. The first question I usually ask on the Invitation Sheet is "What initially drew you to the poem?" To the group directly, I might add "Was it the title, the perceived subject? Some poems attracted you. Some didn't. What interested you in the poem you selected? Poems are made of language. Something in the language attracted you."

The second question on the Invitation Sheet is "What words, lines, and images stand out for you in your poem?" The third set of questions on the Invitation Sheet is "What about the poem matters to you?" and "Why did you pick it?" The final question is "How does the poem intersect with your life and work?"

A good question in a Poetry Table experience is open-ended and gives people the space to think. The questions are a catalyst for conversation. Four or five open-ended questions are enough, although I have tried as many as six. Three seems too few.

The questions I typically ask on the Invitation Sheet aren't about solving problems. They are about personal meaning and values. For example, I ask "What about the poem matters to you?" "Why did you pick it?" "How does the poem intersect with your life and work?" I am not asking "How does the poem intersect with the problems you are facing in your life and work?" Asking that question would open the door to problem-solving and would likely compel others to want to be helpful and give advice. The conversation that would ensue could turn negative, become exhausting, and de-energizing. I want people to feel energized and inspired.

It is essential to tailor some questions to the group and its context for coming together. For example, for a public servant leader program with a state agency, I changed the fourth question to "How does your poem intersect with your life, work, and being a public servant leader?" Questions ask people to focus on specifics. If I don't include that last part—being a public servant leader—then people will talk about their life and work only. Anything that I want people to think and talk about needs to be asked.

For the state agency group, I added a fifth question, "How does your poem connect with your passion for making a difference as a state employee?" There are, of course, other questions I could ask.

The questions do my work as a facilitator, allowing the group to self-manage. Sometimes, someone in the group will voluntarily take on the role of question-asker guide. Sometimes I ask for a volunteer in the group to do this. The person who takes this role makes sure everyone gets to answer the Invitation Sheet questions, and they keep everyone on track and the conversation going.

A characteristic of a powerful question is that the language can continue working on a person beyond the meeting time and in the most unexpected ways. A prime moment when the work occurs is when the person slows down, such as late at night, when the unconscious is free to visit. The busyness of life during daylight hours has passed. One is left alone with the question and one's thoughts. It may be 2:00 in the morning. The wolf at 2:00 a.m. has arrived.

Poems can also include powerful questions . . .

Harlem

What happens to a dream deferred?
Does it dry up
like a raisin in the sun?
Or fester like a sore—
And then run?
Does it stink like rotten meat?
Or crust and sugar over—
like a syrupy sweet?

Maybe it just sags
like a heavy load.

Or does it explode?

Langston Hughes

"Harlem" is simple and straightforward, and therein lies its power and depth. It's a good example of why it's best to avoid too much analysis, which would shift the focus from the heart to the head and take away from the power of the carefully constructed words. Saying less is more.

"A paradigm shift occurs when a question is asked inside the current paradigm that can only be answered from outside it."

Marilee Goldberg Adams, *The Art of the Question*

Change starts with the individual. The poem and then the following discussion help facilitate change. An essential design element for a facilitator is to focus on constructing the right questions, rather than worry about the answers. A good design includes compelling questions.

Questions can open the door to self-discovery and dialogue. Group members discover things they didn't know about the person speaking. This valuable practice extends far beyond a Poetry Table.

THE FACILITATOR'S ROLE DURING SMALL GROUPS

After the small groups leave for their breakout areas, I'll walk around and briefly listen in on each group just to see how the conversation is going and get a flavor for what is happening. I just slowly walk by three or four times. I almost never sit with a group.

I don't want to be intrusive or disrupt their conversation, their intimate "bubble" if they are in one. I only pick up snippets of the stories and conversations, noting on a piece of paper the poems people have picked. I might only catch the names of one or two. Later, as they are wrapping up the appreciations, which I'll discuss below, I'll ask everyone what they picked. I write them down and put the paper in the folder I have for the group. I like to keep a record of the poems for two reasons. The primary one is so I can ask group members to read their poems and then talk about them at later sessions. A second reason is to have a sense of the poems that are popular. As I find new poems, I might add them to my Poetry Table stacks and remove ones that don't get chosen.

APPRECIATIONS

At the end of a Poetry Table, before each small group finishes up and returns to the large group, I encourage people to share appreciations. "What did someone say that made a difference to you? What did you appreciate?" With this, I am supporting or reinforcing an attitude of gratitude. I encourage people to be specific and detailed in their appreciations. For example, "When you shared that story about your fear of leaving your job and starting your own business, I could really relate to you and relate to your fear. I am at a crossroads, too, and am thinking of leaving my job."

It can be life changing to know how we impact others. Sometimes we are blind to our gifts, however well we may know our deficiencies and weaknesses. We've heard them all our lives from parents, in school, and in performance evaluations at work. "Here is the difference you made for me." It is important to say and hear it. Such information can be energizing, inspirational, and transformative.

LARGE GROUP

Back in the large group after their small-group experience, I ask people, "What was valuable for you about that experience, from reading the poems in silence, to picking one, to reading yours and talking about it, to hearing others read theirs and talk about theirs?" Large group sharing brings everyone together and creates respect and appreciation for the larger entity.

I once heard author and consultant Peter Block say, "The small group is the unit of transformation within the larger entity" because of the intimacy of the small group dynamic. In my experience, this is true. The small group is where some of the action is and where change takes place. It is where people can find their voice, be heard, and where even the most reticent or marginalized person can find human connection. But small groups can become tribal. It is important to bring people together into one large group and remind them that we are bigger than the small groups.

After we discuss the value of the experience, I'll ask, "Who would like to read their poem, say why they picked it, why it matters to them, and how it intersects with their life and work?" My rule of thumb is three poem readings and sharings at a time. After three, group members start losing focus. The poems and sharing of three people are enough to absorb.

It's often powerful for people to read their poems in the large group and talk about why they chose their selection. Sharing in front of a larger audience, a greater gathering of humanity, can be a bolder act. It is usually at this point that I hear why a person chose a poem, why it matters, and how it intersects with their life and work.

Both small and large groups are necessary. There's the intimate, immediate experience of sharing the poem in the small group. And then, when we reconvene in the large group, people courageously share in front of the full community.

TRANSITION POINTS AND CLOSING

To keep the poetry alive and for going deep fast, I usually have people read to the large group at transition points in multi-day programs, before or after breaks, before or after lunch, and at the end of the day, almost as a benediction. This weaves purpose, depth, and meaning throughout a program.

Depending on the program length and frequency, a month or several months may have passed after people first read their poems.

Some immediacy is lost over time. Sometimes people struggle to remember why they picked the poem. I give people advance notice that I'd like for them to read their chosen poem so they can recall why they selected it or, if they can't recall, then they can relate it to their current moment.

I send the email invitation a week or so before the training and then a reminder maybe a day or two before. Most of the time people have their poem on their phone. If they don't, I send them a link to find it.

During an all-day session, I might have two to three people read and share after the morning break and two to three read and share after lunch, or I might do it before lunch and before we end. I don't have a set way and time. It depends on the other activities and their timing, the energy of the group, the larger program context, and what feels right at the time.

Reading the poems after breaks is beneficial because people invariably check their emails or make work calls. The poems refocus the participants, re-grounds them in meaning and purpose. The participants have to pay attention and listen closely.

Although I want to eventually give everyone the opportunity to read and talk, I need to think about when to email and ask quieter people to read. It's mostly a guess from experience. I tend to ask the more reserved people at a later session.

I am sensitive to how willing someone is to read and talk in front of the large group. If I ask too soon, I risk them saying they are uncomfortable reading. I certainly allow people to decline to read and talk to the large group. Choice is honored. People can say no because of the delicate nature of what the poem means to them, or for any other reason. They don't have to tell me. They might not be comfortable taking the risk in the large group. I respect their decision.

The quieter ones are often the most powerful speakers because the group hasn't heard their voices much, if at all. Most of the more reserved people will eventually speak, and when they do, their words are concise and powerful.

More often the people who don't want to speak in front of the group are uncomfortable and may fear becoming emotional. It can be helpful to have the poem to read. The poem takes some attention from the reader. Without the poem, the reader might feel more exposed, the center of attention. People who might not be willing to speak directly about what matters to them for three minutes, will, with the poem in hand, speak about why the poem matters to them and how it intersects with their lives. So, in essence, they are talking about themselves.

In addition to sharing more of who they are with the group, it gives people practice in public speaking without having to give a speech.

After the engineer who lost his son to suicide spoke, I thanked him. It is all I usually say out of respect for their sharing. A brief expression of appreciation and silence is better than a bunch of noisy words from me that clutter the impact or shift the focus to me. The focus needs to stay on the speaker and the profound moment that has been created.

Sometimes group members clap after their classmates read and share. I take the clapping as a spontaneous appreciation of their classmates' courageous, heartfelt speech. Usually, the comments come across as genuine and unrehearsed. Just human.

VIRTUAL AND IN-PERSON POETRY TABLES

Consider me old school regarding in-person versus virtual Poetry Tables. As Naomi Shihab Nye said in "Red Brocade," which I shared in the Introduction, "I refuse to be claimed."

While I recognize the time-saving and travel-saving benefits of virtual training, too many things are lost in a digital environment that are gained by in-person Poetry Tables. An in-person experience allows for a fuller sensory and emotional experience. In the virtual world, of our five senses, only sight and hearing are engaged. By being in the actual presence of others, more of your senses are engaged, and sight and hearing are even more fully engaged.

And then there is the issue of communication and body language. We communicate nonverbally through conscious and unconscious gestures and movements. Some studies show that as much of 93% of communication occurs through nonverbal behavior and tone and only 7% of communication takes place through the use of words.

Even if you set aside the studies, facts, and percentages, there is something tangible, important, and real about holding a piece of paper with a poem on it in your hand. All of these things make an in-person Poetry Table conversation the desired medium.

CHAPTER 19

More "Whys" Behind Poetry Tables

"I really do believe literature is an empathy tool, and reading literature widely can actually make you an empathetic person."[5]

Sarah Levine, a professor at the Stanford Graduate School of Education.

A POETRY TABLE TEACHES empathy. In a society that doesn't read enough, where there are so many distractions, we forget that the study of literature is the best and oldest tool for developing emotional understanding. You get a taste of this with a Poetry Table. In many classrooms, the structure of standardized tests, especially multiple-choice questions and narrow essay rubrics, pushes teachers to drill students on finding arguments and literary devices rather than encouraging them to reflect on their emotional response. "The standardized testing movement reduces literary reading to fact-finding," Ms. Levine has said.[6]

Reading literature, including poetry, helps you to imagine other people's lives. A Poetry Table is a great way for strangers to open up to

5. Sarah Levine, "The Trouble with Empathy," *The New York Times*, September 4, 2020, https://www.nytimes.com/2020/09/04/opinion/sunday/empathy-school-college.html.
6. Levine, "The Trouble with Empathy."

each other, for people of different genders, races, or cultures to experience common humanity.

Knowing someone's story creates empathy. Understanding another person's story can shift how you see their actions or reduce unfair and inaccurate behavioral assumptions. Hearing someone's story can create a new level of respect and caring for other people.

You don't have to connect with everyone in the small group to feel less isolated and have a sense of belonging. Connecting to one person can be enough. Any human connection can make you feel more connected to the larger group. That sense of belonging may stick with you when you exit the room and enter the world. When you feel more connected, you will be kinder and more compassionate.

Poetry Tables can be used to introduce students to poetry. Entire curricula could be written about using Poetry Tables in different classroom settings. For example, the chosen poems could focus on a single poet as a way to introduce students to his or her work. The poems could be selected to highlight a period of poetry, a type of poetry, or particular themes. There is no limit to the arrangements.

I have done Poetry Tables in fifth-grade classrooms, kindergarten classrooms, and adult continuing education classrooms. In continuing education classes, after the small-group Poetry Table experience, longer poems can be examined and discussed. We have time to talk about the allusions and references if students want to.

In a multi-class format, whether it is in an elementary school or college, the students have time to read the poem before the next class. Therefore, they have time to think about and reflect on a poem before it's discussed.

The truth is, Poetry Tables have unlimited outcomes. A Poetry Table could be designed to focus on any topic.

CHAPTER 20

Last Heartfelt Words

IT IS FITTING TO end on a poem of radiance, imaginative promise, serendipity, and wonder of the realm. Here is a favorite of mine by Irish Poet and Nobel Prize winner, Seamus Heaney.

Postscript

And some time make the time to drive out west
Into County Clare, along the Flaggy Shore,
In September or October, when the wind
And the light are working off each other
So that the ocean on one side is wild
With foam and glitter, and inland among stones
The surface of a slate-grey lake is lit
By the earthed lightning of a flock of swans,
Their feathers roughed and ruffling, white on white,
Their fully-grown headstrong-looking heads
Tucked or cresting or busy underwater.
Useless to think you'll park or capture it
More thoroughly. You are neither here nor there,
A hurry through which known and strange things pass
As big soft buffetings come at the car sideways
And catch the heart off guard and blow it open.

Seamus Heaney

APPENDIX

SAMPLE EXPECTATIONS OF
POETRY TABLE FACILITATORS – SUMMARY

A facilitator has multiple roles and functions to perform throughout a Poetry Table. Each facilitator is responsible for providing the participant group with the following basic elements:

Choice: It is important to emphasize that no one will be forced to read, but rather a Poetry Table is an opportunity, and each participant may exercise choice at any point.

Safety: It is critical to talk about safety and establish it before running a Poetry Table. The facilitator is responsible for creating a container within the group that is emotionally and psychologically safe. If people perceive that there is real risk involved then a great deal of reasonable resistance will emerge.

Purpose: Provide the contextual framework of the program.

Process: The primary process of the course is experiential learning. A Poetry Table is an opportunity to learn about oneself, others, teamwork, leadership, and community.

Outcomes: The outcomes of a Poetry Table will be new insights, which will help the individual and group work together in a better fashion. It will help them pull together and learn to utilize teamwork as a springboard for facing the challenges of the future.

SAMPLE QUALITIES OF A
POETRY TABLE FACILITATOR – SUMMARY

In addition to the positive attributes discussed in chapter 14, the following qualities of a Poetry Table facilitator are also important.

The professionalism of Poetry Table facilitators is critical to their effectiveness with participants. Facilitators are encouraged to address personal issues that could potentially influence their work with participants. There is no one best "type" of facilitator. There are however some characteristics and skills that enable facilitators to be more effective. Poetry Table facilitators are expected to develop and strengthen the following qualities:

Trustworthiness: It is important for facilitators to have the respect and trust of individuals and the group.

Competency: It is critical for facilitators to know what they are talking about and to be able to do what they say they will do.

Flexibility: Facilitators should strive to adopt the rhythm and rhyme of the group, class, or team. They are there to serve the needs of the group, not vice versa.

Openness: It is important for facilitators to look for new ways to see and to hear. If they are asking their participants to look at the world through different lenses, then they must be willing to do the same.

Integrity: Facilitators must commit to act honestly in accordance with their personal and group values. They are expected to follow through with commitments they have made with the group.

Honesty: It is important for facilitators to admit to their mistakes. Honesty creates trust and certainty. Dishonesty generates uncertainty and mistrust. Honesty builds integrity.

Sense of Humor: Facilitators should be able to laugh at themselves. If anyone takes himself or herself too seriously, it interferes with learning from others.

Learner Mentality: The ability of a facilitator to be a role model can be a great asset. They should be open to learning from others. Each Poetry Table is a learning opportunity. This is the gateway to continuous improvement.

Sense of Timing: It is critical that facilitators are aware of when it is right to listen, to speak, to intervene, and to disappear. Good intuition is as valuable as common sense.

Enthusiastic: It is crucial that facilitators are interested and engaged in what they are doing. Poetry Table facilitators need to care about poetry!

Willingness to Accept Differences: Facilitators are expected to accept and honor diversity of all types. Diversity and inclusively are essential for creativity and innovation.

SAMPLE OF THE INVITATION SHEET

The Invitation

From your stack, please select the poem that resonates with you and which you like the most.

Please take your turn. You are invited to read your poem **TWICE,** slowly, to your group and then answer the questions:

- What initially drew you to the poem?
- What words, lines, and images stand out for you in your poem?
- What about the poem matters to you? Why did you pick it?
- How does the poem intersect with your life and work?

This is not high school English where poetry may have been about analysis and right and wrong answers. There are NO RIGHT or WRONG answers to these questions. Your answers reflect what you believe and speak to your experience with the poem.

Group members can ask questions and talk to the speaker who is taking her turn. It is meant that you will talk to each other and have a conversation about the poem. But please make sure everyone gets her turn and gets to answer ALL the questions.

In closing, before returning to the large group, after everyone has read and talked about their poems, please tell each other what you appreciated about the conversation. What did others say that mattered to you?

Tell each other in specific terms.

LISTS OF POEMS

As I mention several times in the text, a single poem could appeal to a range of people of different ages, cultures, backgrounds, etc. For example, the poem "Don't Quit" could appeal to many humans who are struggling and persevering, universal things humans do.

I am almost reluctant to give a list and exclude a poem. The truth is one never knows what a human will pick. The listing of potential good poems to use could be a book in itself. However, I recognize it is helpful for facilitators and educators new to Poetry Tables to have a starter list—so here goes!

Poems with Internet Links

"So Much Happiness" by Naomi Shihab Nye
https://poets.org/poem/so-much-happiness

"Shoulders" by Naomi Shihab Nye
https://poets.org/poem/shoulders

"Kindness" by Naomi Shihab Nye
https://poets.org/poem/kindness

"Gate A-4" by Naomi Shihab Nye
https://poets.org/poem/gate-4

"Red Brocade" by Naomi Shihab Nye
https://poets.org/poem/red-brocade

"Famous" by Naomi Shihab Nye
https://poets.org/poem/famous

"Making a Fist" by Naomi Shihab Nye
https://poets.org/poem/making-fist

"Lost" by David Wagoner
https://www.poetryfoundation.org/poetrymagazine/browse?contentId=31967

"Still I Rise" by Maya Angelou
https://poets.org/poem/still-i-rise

"The Road Not Taken" by Robert Frost
https://poets.org/poem/road-not-taken

"Mending Wall" by Robert Frost
https://poets.org/poem/mending-wall

"I dwell in Possibility" (466) by Emily Dickinson
https://www.poetryfoundation.org/
poems/52197/i-dwell-in-possibility-466

"Hope is the thing with feathers" (314) by Emily Dickinson
https://www.poetryfoundation.org/poems/42889/
hope-is-the-thing-with-feathers-314

"Much Madness is divinest Sense" (620) by Emily Dickinson
https://www.poetryfoundation.org/poems/51612/
much-madness-is-divinest-sense-620

"Success is counted sweetest" (112) by Emily Dickinson
https://www.poetryfoundation.org/poems/45721/
success-is-counted-sweetest-112

"Tell all the truth but tell it slant" (1263) by Emily Dickinson
https://www.poetryfoundation.org/poems/56824/
tell-all-the-truth-but-tell-it-slant-1263

"Archaic Torso of Apollo" by Rainer Maria Rilke
https://poets.org/poem/archaic-torso-apollo

"Introduction to Poetry" by Billy Collins
https://www.poetryfoundation.org/poems/46712/
introduction-to-poetry

"Aimless Love" by Billy Collins
https://www.poetryfoundation.org/poetrymagazine/
browse?contentId=41392

"A Ritual To Read to Each Other" by William Stafford
https://www.poetryfoundation.org/
poems/58264/a-ritual-to-read-to-each-other

"Late Ripeness" by Czeslaw Milosz
https://www.poetryfoundation.org/poems/49453/late-ripeness

"To Be of Use" by Marge Piercy
https://www.poetryfoundation.org/poems/57673/to-be-of-use

"Eagle Poem" by Joy Harjo

https://www.poetryfoundation.org/poems/46545/eagle-poem

"Mother to Son" by Langston Hughes
https://www.poetryfoundation.org/poems/47559/mother-to-son

"Harlem" by Langston Hughes
https://www.poetryfoundation.org/poems/46548/harlem

"Let Evening Come" by Jane Kenyon
https://www.poetryfoundation.org/poems/46431/let-evening-come

"Invictus" by William Ernest Henley
https://www.poetryfoundation.org/poems/51642/invictus

"From Blossoms" by Li-Young Lee
https://www.poetryfoundation.org/poems/43012/from-blossoms

"One Art" by Elizabeth Bishop
https://www.poetryfoundation.org/poems/47536/one-art

"For the Anniversary of My Death" by W.S. Merwin
https://www.poetryfoundation.org/poems/43118/
for-the-anniversary-of-my-death

"The Layers" by Stanley Kunitz
https://www.poetryfoundation.org/poems/54897/the-layers

"The Second Coming" by William Butler Yeats
https://www.poetryfoundation.org/poems/43290/the-second-coming

Other Poems, Poetic Quotes, and Excerpts of Poetic Language

"The Journey," "Wild Geese," "When Death Comes," "The Summer Day," and "Magellan" by Mary Oliver

From "Andrea del Sarto" by Robert Browning

"The Art of Disappearing" by Naomi Shihab Nye

"It's This Simple" by Hugh Prather

"Hope" by Lisel Mueller

From "Earth, Fire, and Water" by William Butler Yeats

"Patient Trust" by Pierre Telhard de Chardin

"Life is a Garden" by Bokanon

"Fire," "Trough," and "Wooden Boats" by Judy Brown

"The Grasp of Your Hand" and "Where the Mind Is Without Fear" by Rabindranath Tagore

"Listen" by James Autry

"The Avowal" by Denise Levertov

"The Invitation" by Oriah Mountain Dreamer

"Courage" by Amelia Earhart

"Sometimes" by Sheenagh Pugh

"The Real Work," "A Vision," and "A Purification" by Wendell Berry

"There Was a Time I Would Reject Those" by Muhyiddin Ibn Arabi

"Postscript" by Seamus Heaney

"To Find Our Place of Leading" by Martin Challis

"When Someone Deeply Listens to You" by John Fox

"It Is I Who Must Begin" by Vaclav Havel

"The Guest House," "Love Dogs," "The Lame Goat," and "There Is a Field" by Jellaludin Rumi

"Fluent" by John O'Donohue

"Keeping Quiet" by Pablo Neruda

From "Auguries of Innocence" by William Blake

"Faith," "Hope," "Love," and "On Prayer" by Czeslaw Milosz

"Autobiography in Five Short Chapters" by Portia Nelson

"No te salves/Don't Save Yourself" by Mario Benedetti

"The Seven of Pentacles" by Marge Piercy

"How Do I Listen" by Hafiz

"Courage" by Anne Sexton

From "The Drum Major Instinct" by Dr. Martin Luther King, Jr.

"Now I Become Myself" by May Sarton

"Don't Quit" by Edgar Guest

"Imperfection" by Elizabeth Carlson

"The Wolf at Two A.M.," "Accounting," "To The Animal Not Roadkill," "The Stream," and "White Hearse" by David Markwardt

"I Am Not I" by Juan Ramon Jimenez

"Optimism," "Against Certainty," and "Bees" by Jane Hirshfield

"Hook" by James Wright

"Love After Love" by Derek Walcott

From "Little Gidding" by T.S. Elliot

"The Uses of Not" by Lao Tzu

"A Story That Could be True," "With Kit, Age 7 At the Beach," "You Reading This, Be Ready," "Silver Star," and "The Way It is" by William Stafford

"A Note," "Nothing's a Gift," "Could Have," "Possibilities," "A Few Words on the Soul," and "A Contribution to Statistics" by Wislawa Szymborska

"Gift" by Czeslaw Milosz

"Work Around Your Abyss" by Henri Nouwen

AN EXERCISE FOR YOU

Find a private, quiet place. Go back and read the poems in the book. After you have read them all, please select the poem which resonates with you and which you like the most.

Even though you are alone, please read your poem out loud **TWICE,** slowly, and then journal your responses to the following four questions:

- What initially drew you to the poem?
- What words, lines, and images, stand out for you in your poem?
- What about the poem matters to you? Why did you pick it?
- How does the poem intersect with your life and work?

THE INVITATION:
EMAIL ME A LINK TO YOUR FAVORITE POEM

I am always on the search for compelling and interesting poems and to learn about poets I don't know. I knew nothing about Polish poetry until I decided to teach a continuing education course at Santa Fe Community College on poets who had won the Nobel Prize in Literature. In teaching that course, I became familiar with the poetry of Czeslaw Milosz and Wislawa Szymborska. They've become favorite poets.

Please email me (davidbmarkwardt@gmail.com) a link to your favorite poems. It's how I keep learning too!

If you care to share a note with the poem, perhaps answer the following questions:

- What draws you to the poem?
- What words, lines, and images stand out for you in the poem?
- What about it matters?
- How does the poem intersect with your life and work?

Thank you!

David Markwardt has a Master of Science in Organization Development from Pepperdine University, a Master of Fine Arts in Poetry from Vermont College of Norwich University, and a B.A. from Dartmouth College. He is also a published poet. He has been leading team, leadership, and community programs for thirty years. Poetry Tables are a manifestation of many academic and professional threads in his life. He lives in Lamy, New Mexico, outside of Santa Fe.

COPYRIGHTS AND PERMISSIONS

The Red Book (Philemon) 1st Edition by C. G. Jung (Author), Sonu Shamdasani (Editor, Translator), Mark Kyburz (Translator), John Peck (Translator).

Kolb, D. A. (1984). *Experiential learning: Experience as the source of learning and development* (Vol. 1). Englewood Cliffs, NJ: Prentice-Hall.

Poem credits are listed in the order that they appear in the book.

"Red Brocade" from pp. 82-83 in *Everything Comes Next* by Naomi Shihab Nye - Read By: Naomi Shihab Nye, James Patrick Cronin. *Everything Comes Next: Collected and New Poems*, Copyright © 1994, 1995, 1998, 2000, 2001, 2002, 2004, 2005, 2008, 2011, 2018, 2019, 2020 by Naomi Shihab Nye. Used by permission of HarperCollins Publishers.

"Lost" from *Traveling Light: Collected and New Poems* by David Wagoner. Copyright © 1999 by David Wagoner. Used with permission of the poet and the University of Illinois Press.

"Some People Like Poetry" from *Poems New and Collected* by Wislawa Szymborska. Copyright © by The Wislawa Szymborska Foundation. English language copyright © 1998 by HarperCollins Publishers. Used by permission of HarperCollins Publishers.

"Courage" from *The Awful Rowing Toward God* by Anne Sexton. Copyright © 1975 by Loring Conant, Jr., Executor of the Estate of Anne Sexton. Used by permission of HarperCollins Publishers and SLL/Sterling Lord Literistic, Inc. Copyright by Linda Gray Sexton, Literary Executor for Anne Sexton.

"Kindness" from *Words Under the Words: Selected Poems* by Naomi Shihab Nye. Copyright © 1995 by Naomi Shihab Nye. Reprinted with permission from Far Corner Books, Portland, Oregon.

"Don't Quit" (poet unknown): Every effort has been made to identify and locate copyright holder for this work. The publisher would be grateful for further information concerning this author/rightsholder. Any errors or omissions will be corrected in subsequent editions.

"My Intention" by Czeslaw Milosz, is an excerpt from pp. 1-2 in *To Begin Where I Am, Selected Essays* by Czeslaw Milosz. Edited and with an Introduction by Bogdana Carpenter and Madeline G. Levine. Copyright © 2001 by Czeslaw Milosz. Published by Farrar Straus and Giroux.

"You Reading This, Be Ready" from *Ask Me: 100 Essential Poems* by William Stafford. Copyright © 1980, 1991, 1989, 2014 by William Stafford and the Estate of William Stafford. Reprinted with the permission of The Permissions Company, LLC on behalf of Graywolf Press, Minneapolis, Minnesota, graywolfpress.org

"Imperfection" by Elizabeth Carlson is reprinted with permission from the poet's estate.

"Now I Become Myself" from *Collected Poems 1930-1993* by May Sarton. Copyright © 1974 by May Sarton. Used by permission of W. W. Norton & Company, Inc. and Russell & Volkening as agents for the Estate of May Sarton.

"I Am Not I" from *Lorca & Jimenez: Selected Poems* by Juan Ramon Jimenez. Chosen and Translated by Robert Bly. Copyright © 1973 by Robert Bly. Copyright © 1967 by The Sixties Press. Reprinted with permission from Beacon Press. Permission conveyed through Copyright Clearance Center, Inc.

"Archaic Torso of Apollo" by Rainer Maria Rilke. Translation copyright © 1982 by Stephen Mitchell; from *Selected Poetry of Rainer Maria Rilke* by Rainer Maria Rilke, edited and translated by Stephen Mitchell. Used by permission of Random House, an imprint and division of Penguin Random House LLC. All rights reserved.

"The Way It Is" from *Ask Me: 100 Essential Poems* by William Stafford. Copyright © 1980, 1991, 1989, 2014 by William Stafford and the Estate of William Stafford. Reprinted with the permission of The Permissions Company, LLC on behalf of Graywolf Press, Minneapolis, Minnesota, graywolfpress.org

"A Few Words on the Soul" from *Monologue of a Dog* by Wislawa Szymborska. Copyright © by The Wislawa Szymborska Foundation. Translation copyright © 2006 by HarperCollins Publishers. Used by permission of HarperCollins Publishers.

"Gift" from *Collected Poems* by Czeslaw Milosz. Copyright © 1988 by Czeslaw Milosz Royalties, Inc. Used by permission of HarperCollins Publishers.

"Late Ripeness" from *Second Space: New Poems* by Czeslaw Milosz. Translated by the author and Robert Hass. Copyright © 2004 by Czeslaw Milosz. Translation copyright © 2004 by Robert Hass. Used by permission of HarperCollins Publishers and The Wylie Agency LLC.

"Hook" from *Above the River: The Complete Poems* by James Wright, introduction by Donald Hall. Copyright 1990 by Anne Wright, introduction © 1990 by Donald Hall. Reprinted by permission of Farrar, Straus and Giroux. All Rights Reserved.

"Introduction to Poetry" from *The Apple That Astonished Paris* by Billy Collins. Copyright © 1988, 1996 by Billy Collins. Reprinted with the permission of The Permissions Company, LLC Inc., on behalf of the University of Arkansas Press, uapress.com

"Autobiography in Five Short Chapters" from *There's A Hole In My Sidewalk: The Romance of Self-Discovery* by Portia Nelson. Copyright © 1993 by Portia Nelson. Reprinted with the permission of Beyond Words/Atria Books, a division of Simon & Schuster. All rights reserved.

"Against Certainty" from *After* by Jane Hirshfield. Copyright © 2006 by Jane Hirshfield. Used by permission of HarperCollins Publishers. This poem also appears in *The Asking: New & Selected Poems* by Jane Hirshfield. (Bloodaxe Books, 2024) and is reproduced with permission from Bloodaxe Books. www.bloodaxebooks.com. @bloodaxebooks (twitter/facebook) #bloodaxeboo

"With Kit, Age 7, at the Beach" from *Ask Me: 100 Essential Poems* by William Stafford. Copyright © 1980, 1991, 1989, 2014 by William Stafford and the Estate of William Stafford. Reprinted with the permission of The Permissions Company, LLC on behalf of Graywolf Press, Minneapolis, Minnesota, graywolfpress.org

"A Contribution to Statistics" from *Poems New and Collected* by Wislawa Szymborska. Copyright © by The Wislawa Szymborska Foundation. English language copyright ©1998 by HarperCollins Publishers. Used by permission of HarperCollins Publishers.

www.ingramcontent.com/pod-product-compliance
Lightning Source LLC
Chambersburg PA
CBHW071617150726
48000CB00004B/1757